How to Have a Brain Tumour

by

Anne E. Thompson

Published by The Cobweb Press
www.thecobwebpress.com
thecobwebpress@gmail.com

ISBN 978-0-9954632-4-0

For Bob Beffins

Chapter One

Diary of a Brain Tumour
Extracts from my diary, written at the time.
Names have been changed.

Saturday 28th March 2009

Today I discovered I had a brain tumour. So *not* what I was expecting for the day.

I went to the hospital suffering from concussion. On Thursday, I banged my head by coming up under the work surface when I was emptying the tumble dryer (as you do). I think I was 'out' for a few seconds, because the next thing I remember was lying on the floor with Kia licking my face. (Kia is my German Shepherd dog — not a child, in case you were concerned!) I had a headache all afternoon, so a friend took me to the doctor's. He said to see how I was, and to go to hospital if it got worse. I became slightly confused on Friday, and then waking with a headache again today, it seemed prudent to get it checked out. So David drove me to our local A&E and we duly waited in various lines until I was given a CT scan.

By the time the results came my head was pretty awful and I just wanted to go home.

Hospitals are such strange places. You lie on a plastic bed, separated from strangers by a curtain, unable to avoid listening to their most intimate conversations. I heard an old lady talking to a man, who was apologising for being a nuisance (I assume he was her husband) and it made me feel quite tearful.

"You look after me," she said, "and I look after you, and that's just the way it is."

Such honest humanity, such real problems and real love. People stop pretending in hospitals, we're all the same really.

Anyway, there I was with a coat over my head to keep out the light and David beside me, refusing to go home and tapping quietly on his Blackberry. The doctor, a competent and heavily pregnant woman, sat next to me on the bed and showed me the written report from my scan. I was grateful for that — her relaxed approach, and letting me *read* rather than be *told*. It gave me a second to take it in, there's no need to react to a written report in the same way that you have to if you're told something.

I read it twice.

It said I had a colloid cyst in the third ventricle. This meant nothing to me.

The doctor said it was a growth, but assured me that it was not cancerous. She said I needed to see a neurologist and would be referred to one by my GP. She wasn't able to tell me anything else. When I started to ask questions, she just said she didn't know, but I should get it checked.

I was mainly just relieved that my bump hadn't caused anything nasty and that I could go home. I wanted to take my headache to bed.

Driving home, we discussed the cyst, and whether or not to tell the family. In some ways it seems sensible to say nothing until I have seen the neurologist and can tell them something definite. On the other hand, I want them to trust me in the future and not worry that I'm withholding information. I do think the most frightening thing is 'not knowing'. So, I decided that I'd tell them, keeping everything in the open and very calm and sensible. No 'what ifs' just the fact that I have a cyst and it needs to be checked.

We, of course, have absolutely no idea what 'having a cyst' means. I'm sure I've heard somewhere that many people have cysts in their brains, and never know about them because they don't do any harm. Am hoping that's the kind I've got.

All went well until mid afternoon. I was calm, resigned to another possible hospital trip but still just happy that there was no cancer involved. Then Betty decided to do some internet research. I had intended to do this anyway and it was fun doing it together, lying on my bed with her lap top (which she wont let me touch in case I break it).

We discovered that I have a rare form of tumour and the various symptoms. Apparently a 'cyst' is known in medical speak as a 'benign tumour'. That makes it sound a little more scary.

Of all brain tumours (which themselves are rare) colloid cysts are thought to be less than 1%. Am not sure if that makes me special, or especially unlucky. They are tiny, colloid (fat) filled cysts, that are usually found in the third ventricle of the brain. It sounds sort of dirty, I don't know why. I don't want to have a 'fat filled cyst' in me. It makes me think about pus-filled blisters and all things yukky.

The 'third ventricle' is the middle, apparently. Right in the middle.

We read lists of symptoms, though apparently it's possible to have a cyst with no symptoms at all. They are formed before you're born, so I've lived with mine without even knowing it's been there.

John joined us and was amused that memory loss was associated with it—he's sure this explains all my lapses of concentration that make me late for things. Not sure if that's better or worse than being viewed as a bit scatty.

Then they looked up treatment. This seemed rather unpleasant and much more major than I had anticipated. It looks like they basically take off the top of your head and slice through your brain to remove the tumour. Great. I had hoped for aspiration via a needle at worse, non intervention at best. It seems that non intervention results in death, so maybe that's a non option.

Operations look horribly complicated, and result in a whole range of awful side effects. Do I want to be mute? Have memory loss? Be epileptic? It is rather hard to imagine incorporating those little gems into my life. To not remember times spent with David? To never remember my Dad? To not remember the feel of my babies when I held them? No. I wouldn't be me any more.

Time to stop thinking and walk the dog now.

*

Now it is evening. I am left with a rather unsettled feeling of facing the unknown. I do have a sense that perhaps this scan was meant to happen. You see, I went to the doctor a while ago with weird headaches and he checked me thoroughly and said not to worry. I had started having funny headaches, waking every morning with them and not being able to get rid of them. Not agonising, 'lie in bed all day' ones, but enough to make life a bit grim. Plus the forgetting things, not feeling quite 'on top' of life, even though I've cut back my teaching hours by loads.

I did wonder, well, half-wondered, back then, if I could've had something wrong with my brain. So I went to the doctor, slightly embarrassed, and asked if it was possible. He did lots of co-ordination based tests, ran a pin along my foot, asked questions—then told me no, definitely no tumour.

Now a scan had showed what had been missed previously. I've always had migraines occasionally, but not like my current headaches, so I wonder if the cyst has changed. Do they grow?

I do not know how serious a condition this is. I have a tumour of 8mm diameter. Is that teeny and needs no attention unless it grows to 30mm? Or is it dangerously huge and needs to be operated on within the week? It is very strange to not know something so major. I read a few reports online about colloid cysts only being found post-mortem, that they often cause 'sudden instant death'. Until recently, when people started to have scans, they were only ever found because they killed people. What am I supposed to do with that knowledge?

So, we got take-out food and carried on as normal. I slunk out to email my sister and to write this. It seems to help, to not ignore it but also to not scaremonger. What a strange day this has been.

Sunday 29th March

Had a truly awful night! How does one stop thinking through every possibility and trying to solve it? The whole not-knowing-what-I'm-dealing-with is impossible for me. I planned whole talks, requests for healing, wrote books and chose a headscarf for if my hair is shaved. My funeral is sorted…

At church felt tired and tearful but think it was okay. I didn't actually crack up, though I felt as fragile as glass. I spoke briefly to someone after the service. She seemed fairly unconcerned, was in a rush and hardly listening.

Guess I have to get used to that, what is consuming all my thoughts and energy right now really does not particularly affect other people. I feel like the whole world has changed, but for everyone else, it's just a normal day. Another reason I guess for not rushing to tell people because I know that if they know, I will expect them to care. And they might not.

I did tell another close friend, who of course was lovely, caring and positive.

I want to put life 'on hold' for a bit until I know what to expect. The not knowing is very hard.

Very tired, hard to carry on as normal. David is my absolute rock, I could not go through anything without him. I lean on him very heavily.

Sunday 5th April

Went to the GP on Monday. I decided to go early and stand in line, rather than phone for an appointment. Not very cool but I want this thing sorted.

Dr B had never heard of it, he knew less than me. I tried asking my list of questions, (I had written them all down so I wouldn't forget). But he just said he didn't know and I needed to ask a neurologist. I referred briefly to my visit of last year when I had gone to ask if I had a brain tumour due to weird symptoms (and left feeling silly) but he didn't pick up on it. I don't know if he'll include that information in his letter to neurologist, or if they will think this all started with the CT scan. He advised me to use BUPA, because apparently it can take months to see a neurologist, so I phoned David, who sorted that.

Then I waited and waited. Have heard nothing *all week.*

Have read lots, some articles suggesting nothing needs to be done but regular monitoring, others stating that this is dangerous and needs to be sorted out. The ones that scare me are case studies of patients who had only minor headaches when they went to bed, but then died during the night. Apparently most colloid cysts are found post mortem, because they don't cause the 'normal' brain tumour symptoms (so my doctor didn't miss anything when he checked me, there was nothing to indicate something was wrong). Most of what I'm reading I barely understand anyway. Lots of talk about ventricles and spinal fluid and hydrocephalus—which I have a vague idea about but nothing concrete.

I am worn out. I am not sleeping and it is pretty much constantly on my mind (ha ha!)

I just want to talk to someone who knows about it. I want to ask if my symptoms are related to the tumour and can be sorted out, or if they are just due to age and hormones. If nothing needs to be done, I want to be convinced of this by an intelligent, informed person, not just friends offering reassuring platitudes.

David and kids remain wonderfully sane. I have told several friends, mainly because it felt like lying to say I was fine when they ask how I am. My mother-in-law phoned me, then came yesterday with some tulips. Mum is worried and has made herself ill. She's on antibiotics for a sore throat and has friends visiting her, so goodness knows WHAT she has been telling people. I don't really know what to tell her, because I don't know myself. My sister has emailed a few times. A friend rang and had a nice chat. Other people seem totally unconcerned and disinterested.

Life however, continues as normal. I took Monday off work, partly to visit the doctor but mainly because of weird head from concussion. Worked Thursday.

Saturday we had forty people from church here for Chinese take-away and DVD. Was very nice to have something else to focus on (though the morning getting ready was a struggle as I woke with yet another headache. I hate the 'waking up' ones now because they are the new ones—had them just a few months—and I worry they are tumour linked)

I so want to see someone and get this either sorted out or be reassured that it's nothing. I'm quite brave, I could fight if I knew what I was fighting. Actually, I feel quite angry that I should be informed that I have a brain tumour and then be given no resource to discuss it with anyone. A week has been a long time.

I spoke to a doctor friend, and she said a week was too fast to get an appointment to see a neurologist, I may have to wait a month. (I might implode before then.) She also said that no growth in the brain was properly 'benign' because there isn't any space in brains for anything extra—anything that grows there is likely to cause a problem.

I am also having odd dreams. Dreamt that Dad came to see me, told me not to worry as he and Granny and Grampy are waiting and it'll be fine. Felt very calm when I woke—then rather perturbed!

Another thought I keep having, is whether this is what my cousin died of. I know that he didn't drown, that it was classified as a 'dry drowning' because although he died swimming, there wasn't water in his lungs. They assumed it was heart related but maybe it wasn't, maybe he was one of the "sudden instant death" casualties but this is not something they would spot postmortem. Who knows ? And I can't ASK anyone. It worries me because if a cyst *did* kill him, maybe this *is* genetic. Not sure I could bear for one of the kids to have this.

I cannot sufficiently describe my frustrated impatience. Will be totally mad by the time I finally get to meet neurologist.

Thursday, 9th April

Saw the neurologist yesterday evening. I was sent an appointment for two week's time—*two weeks!*—but the secretary changed it when I phoned and said how worried I was.

(A friend, who has spent lots of time around hospitals with her son, told me that once I have been referred by my GP, I could phone the consultant's office and make the appointment myself. I do not have to wait for them to contact me with a date. Good advice for the future.)

The consultation began by asking lots of questions about the concussion—he seemed to think that was why I was there (am guessing he hadn't read the notes before I got there). It was annoying, because I didn't want to talk about that, I wanted to ask about the cyst, but I didn't know how to politely move him on.

He then listened while I described my headaches and I had written it all down for him, so I gave him my notes. He kept asking how the headaches were different, seemed convinced that everything was due to my migraines, which I've had my whole life. Apparently some brains are susceptible to migraines, and if so, they can do other odd things. This wasn't helpful to know. Plus, I discovered it is *really* difficult to describe a pain.

He checked reflexes, vision, ran a pin down the sole of my foot, etc (none of which are affected by a colloid cyst according to my online research—so were, in my opinion, a waste of time) then told me that the symptoms which I had described were not due to the cyst. Not sure how he would know that.

I asked him some questions, like the percentage of patients with cysts that die. He kept telling me that death from colloid cysts were very rare.

But the cysts themselves are very rare and we know I have one of them! It could be that only 5 cysts will be found all year, but 4 of those people will die.

In the end he admitted that he did not know, they are a rare condition and he had read about them, but couldn't actually answer all my questions. He's never had a patient with a colloid cyst before.

He then went on to refer me to a neurosurgeon, telling me that *he* would know about colloid cysts and would be able to answer my questions. (I've heard that one before.)

In fairness, he was an intelligent bloke and at the time I trusted him and felt reassured by what he said. It's only now, as I reconsider all that I have read, that I am disappointed. I am SURE that the headaches described in every report I have read describe exactly the headaches that I have started getting in the last year. Which, to me, indicates they are linked. The issue seems to be whether or not the colloid cyst is 'symptomatic'. If my headaches and memory lapses are due to the cyst, then it matters. If not, I can stop worrying. I think. All a bit vague to be honest.

I am so scared that the surgeon will read all the reports and decide that there is no need to remove it. I cannot live with this time-bomb inside my head. What if I die while driving the children? Or on the motorway? Or whilst taking a class on an outing? I'm not sure if I can live my life knowing every day that *'sudden instant death'* might be waiting around the corner. (What a horrible phrase *'sudden instant death'* is, and I keep reading it, in nearly every report and case-study I find online. Hard to ignore.)

I want to talk to someone who listens and understands and who has the knowledge to give me good advice. I need to have things thoroughly explained to me because it is so hard trying to understand what I am reading on the internet as I have no perspective to put it into.

I now have to wait another week, at least, due to Easter, before the next step. A week of trying to be normal, trying to sleep and not let all the thoughts that crowd in build up inside my head. A week of calming everyone else who's involved, trying to keep Mum rational, helping prepare the kids for who knows what. This is so hard for me.

Sunday 19th April

Have managed to be relatively normal! The neurologist wasn't able to tell me much, but he had implied I would be having surgery. I therefore decided I may as well tell more people (because I can't keep surgery quiet) so now most people who know me, know as much as me. To be honest, a lot of people seem to have been told anyway, despite me asking the few people who I did tell to not tell other people. Goodness knows what people who heard 'on the grapevine' have been told.

I actually think telling people has been therapeutic. It is a way of dealing with it, getting ready for whatever I need to face. In a way, it's an action in itself, and I need action. As one friend said, I can fight whatever comes against me, but the not-knowing bit makes it impossible to know *what* I'm fighting.

Easter was busy, with people coming here for a walk and cream tea on the Monday. We had about fifty people, and I made the scone dough in the morning, then cooked it in the afternoon while they walked. I like making scones, there is less potential for disaster than with some cooking. Serving lots of people, then clearing up afterwards was good for me. I feel completely drained—would have shattered into a million pieces if anything had gone wrong—but being busy gave me a break from thinking, from the tornado of thoughts circling my mind.

Tuesday I took the kids to Harrods' ice cream parlour. It was fun. Seems it is possible to have fun and laugh, whatever is lurking in your head. The ice-creams are an extortionate price, but you kind of pay for the experience. Afterwards we wandered round the pet department, laughing at all the stupid things people can buy for animals. I can just imagine Kia, our German Shepherd, in a jewel encrusted collar covered in duck poo!

Following my friend's advice, I didn't wait to be contacted by the neurosurgeon, but was proactive and contacted his secretary. I have an appointment tomorrow. Am so worried that he'll want to leave cyst where it is, I really want it to be removed. I feel it was found for a purpose so I want it gone. Soon.

Still not sleeping most nights, think I'm just full of adrenaline.

Friday 24th April

Saw neurosurgeon Monday. Was a bit shell shocked by what he said.

We had to go up to London (David came with me). The hospital is a big old Victorian building, it didn't really feel like a hospital, more like a school. It's right next to the Thames. We went up some steps and into a long waiting room. There were sofas, and a place to get tea and coffee. I could've done with a gin.

We were called in to see the surgeon. He reminded me of a Doctor Who actor from when I was little—lots of energy and a bit quirky, and spoke very fast and completely definite. All he needed was a long scarf and a floppy hat. He was very much in charge of the consultation.

He is also very much against operating, unless cyst is life threatening, because the operation is so risky. He said the risk of leaving someone mute or disabled is high, because to remove the cyst involves damaging the brain. He showed me drawings of the brain, told me that because the cyst is situated right in the middle, he would have to cut through lots of healthy brain, destroying those areas. He pointed repeatedly to a big vein, saying that if it was accidentally nicked during the operation, I would die. He told me he had recently operated on a colleague with a colloid cyst, who was also pregnant, and that she was now very disabled due to a complication with the operation. It was all very scary.

He was a knowledgeable man (knew more than me, anyway—not that that's difficult) and said he had lots of experience of these cysts. He said I may have to live knowing that due to the position of the cyst it cannot be removed. He would know from a MRI scan how life-threatening it was, so at least I would know if likely to die soon or not.

It was not a reassuring visit. Afterwards, we stood outside the hospital, next to the Thames. I just felt numb. I don't even know how to react to what he said.

*

I had the MRI today. I was worried about feeling claustrophobic and it was rather grim but it's done now. I kept my eyes shut, and tried to think about other things. (Actually, I tried to pray, mainly for Anne C, whose cancer has come back, but to be honest, it was just too noisy and I couldn't concentrate. I didn't panic though.)

It was *very* noisy—I did wonder if we'd gone to war (haven't watched the news for a while) and the whole country was being blown up while I was in there. Perhaps I would emerge to find the hospital in ruins around me, only I would've survived due to being enclosed in the machine….

To be honest, one of my main worries was that I might fart. In that enclosed space, there would be no escaping it, and I couldn't pretend it wasn't me when the nurse slid me out amongst a rush of putrid air. But when I finally emerged, all was fine. Everyone still alive, and all gas safely kept inside.

I guess I was in there for about 40 minutes. Before I went in, they injected dye into my arm to show contrast in the images. (When I got home, I told Mum they had put the dye into my ear, and I had to lie on my side until it dripped through my brain and out the other ear. I'm not sure if she believed me, but it made me chuckle.)

David came too, though he had to wait in the waiting room when I was called. It was handy having him there, because I had to strip down to underwear and wear a gown, and he could look after my necklace, earrings and watch. He

14

came because the instructions they sent said I might feel woozy afterwards—I think the dye can make you feel odd. But I was fine. We had lunch next to Thames afterwards, and then he came home with me. It would've been nice, if I wasn't carrying this lump of tension in my tummy all the time.

They didn't tell me what they could see, I have to wait until the neurosurgeon tells me. More waiting.

People are all being very supportive. I received lots of advice before the MRI from people who have had them previously. They told me it would be noisy, I didn't realise *how* noisy. Church people are all praying for me. The staff at school are being supportive and caring. Other parents at school are offering support if I need it, and all being very concerned. It's nice. Feel like I'm seeing the best of people. When God made man He made something good! Sometimes we only see the ruined, selfish, side of people. I feel like I am seeing the warm, kind, wanting to help side that we often don't notice.

Sunday 26th April

We went to watch my brother run in the London Marathon today. I always find it a fairly emotional experience, all those thousands of people putting their energy into doing something for other people. Whether they're supporting or running, it shows the human spirit at its best. Mind you, I'm pretty emotional about everything these days.

Also nice to have a break from thinking about my brain. I am dreading tomorrow (follow up visit to the neurosurgeon). I am so scared he'll just tell me that it's not in a dangerous place and they will monitor it. That sentences me to years of uncertainty, going for tests, wondering if it has grown, trying to monitor my own health—when I want to forget about it and get on with living. It also makes it private, something I have to cope with alone. If there is a physical consequence to this I will get help and support from a multitude of people; if it just stays in my head, if I can still function while it sits there, I have to cope with it on my own. I am tired of coping with things on my own.

David told me that he couldn't sleep last night. He started worrying that the surgeon will say it's critical and whisk me into hospital this week and I'll lose my memory. It's the first time he's told me that he's worried. I don't think for a moment that either of those things will happen, but it was kind of nice to know that this isn't entirely academic for him.

12th May

We saw surgeon. He said the MRI showed the cyst to only be 4mm (despite it being measured as 8mm on the CT scan), and so the risks of operating were too high. Actually, he told me to read that bit of the report aloud—4mm— to reinforce that it was tiny. I felt like a small child being reprimanded, like it was me who had said it was 8mm, and I should've known better.

He will monitor it every six months to see if it's growing but assumes that it won't and that I will live with it forever. He said if I have a huge headache that does not get better then I should get a CT scan done quickly, as fluid may be building up, but he thought that was unlikely to happen.

Cysts usually absorb the dye for the MRI, become 'enhanced', so they're easier to see and measure. My colloid cyst hadn't, even though they had injected me with it, so I asked if he was sure it was a colloid cyst. Initially he said maybe not, then saw that whoever had interpreted the MRI had said it was, so he said that it probably is. He said he couldn't do a biopsy anyway (the only way of knowing for sure) so it was all a case of waiting six months, then having another check. If in six months it has done something unusual, he will reconsider his diagnosis, but for now he is saying it's a colloid cyst. It all felt very uncertain to me.

He again underlined the dangers of operating. He said there would certainly be brain damage and whilst he hoped that would be minor or temporary, he couldn't guarantee either. He did his whole speech again, about how a tiny slip might kill me, and I would probably be left unable to walk, or mute, or with absolutely no memory if I have the operation.

I felt it was all very unsatisfactory. I feel left in limbo, having prepared mentally for surgery and then told it was too risky. I felt I had no say or control in the process, and he listened only to argue back—to convince me of his decision, not to consider any alternative view. He did not seem to believe the headaches I was having were symptomatic, and was under the impression that, had I not had the CT scan, I would never have known about the cyst, and it was therefore all rather a waste of energy. He told me I was a victim of technology, that if I'd never had the CT scan after my bump, I never would've known anything was wrong.

He is only monitoring 2 other patients in my situation (I asked how many other of his patients have colloid cysts—it was the only question he fully answered). I felt he was rather over confident in his own diagnosis as there must surely be some element of doubt when there is so little research on non intervention with these cysts.

I do not know what this has all been about. It felt so 'right' to have a scan and the cyst to be discovered. I was sure that it would be removed, which was confirmed by the neurologist, and I prepared myself accordingly. I feel that I can't trust what seems to be 'right' anymore. Not sure where God is in all this. Why did He give me something to worry about if nothing is going to happen?

November 09

Ages since I wrote in this properly, so I will try to catch up a bit. (It's hard to be consistent with diary writing—and most other things—because when I'm dragging myself through the day with a headache, anything non-essential gets pushed to the bottom of the pile.)

The summer was lovely. I accepted that the cyst was here to stay and all my predictions were wrong. I decided to trust the neurosurgeon, and tried to get on with living. For a while the headaches persisted but throughout August and September I hardly had any at all.

I was disappointed when the hospital rang a week before my next MRI, asking to postpone it. However, I was relaxed enough to arrange the next date for November, after our half term break (six months ago I would have cancelled everything to attend two weeks earlier!) I go next week.

December 09

Follow-up appointment for the MRI was a bit vague—the report said the cyst was 6mm, which means it has grown, but the surgeon said it hadn't, and it had always been about 6mm. (Last time he *definitely* said it was 4mm, so rather confusing.)

At the first consultation I had queried whether that was a single measurement of a solid shape and therefore not necessarily the maximum diameter and he was *absolutely* definite that 4mm was the maximum. At this consultation he gave me a long explanation about solid shapes having different dimensions depending on where they are measured (duh)

When we discussed symptoms, he at first thought there was some evidence of slight hydrocephalus. Then he ruled this out, though did concede that it was possible that my headaches were cyst related. He also listed some further symptoms, like slowing down of thought processes (which I think I do have) and dizziness (which I don't have).

So, we left feeling generally reassured. The cyst is probably causing some problems, but none to worry about. I felt that the cyst had grown but not much. David's understanding was that it had not grown but that the original measurement of 4mm was maybe not accurate.

The radiologist had not had time to do his report for this MRI, with exact measurements, but the neurosurgeon could assure us that there was nothing to worry about. He promised to write after he had received the report. He became a bit vague about whether headaches and memory problems are related or not. However, he was absolutely positive there is no need to operate, it's not life-threatening, no need for any further action for another 6 months.

I do not like the uncertainty of things, but will try to ignore it for another 6 months.

January 2010

An okay day. I dropped the kids at their various bus-stops for school. Phoned vet, and walked dogs on the common. Fed ducks, and sorted Waffle (cat) who still isn't pregnant.

Took dog to vet, made lunch, collected dog from vet.

Did housework. Collected kids.

Made bolognese dinner. Sudden big headache—really huge pain. Took pills, but it didn't go.

Drove John to club, driving slowly due to pain in head. Cleared up dinner. Watched telly.

Bed at 9.30, head still really hurts.

16th Feb 2010

We received a copy of the letter the neurosurgeon sent to the neurologist, following my last consultation. It clearly stated that the cyst was 4mm and static and there were NO symptoms at all. I felt very angry, I felt that the neurosurgeon thought I was lying, or exaggerating, and the whole consultation had been to manage my expectations rather than answering questions with accurate answers. When we were with him, he agreed it was possible that my headaches were linked, now, in his letter to the neurologist, he was denying this. It was almost like he has forgotten the last MRI, and is writing a letter based on the previous one.

I also felt that he had decided very early on, before there was any evidence, that the cyst was static. The neurologist tested things that would be unaffected by a colloid cyst and then told me that it was asymptomatic. The neurosurgeon stated he thought both the symptoms were unrelated **and** that it was static, which was before he had two MRIs to compare. How can you take a single measurement and make a comparative statement? His current letter seemed only to back up his earlier, (in my view unreliable) view. He seemed keen to prove himself right; not to look at the new evidence and make an informed opinion. (Not that his opinion was necessarily wrong, just that it had been reached too quickly and with no evidence.)

While I ranted in futile frustration, David emailed him. Then sent a request for a response. The neurosurgeon emailed back, saying the exact measurements were 6x6x7mm. He felt there was no evidence for any related symptoms and suggested I return to neurologist to discuss cause of headaches.

I felt so angry. I can accept that I may never need an operation but I do need to feel that my questions are being answered and that I am not being 'managed'. I felt that the consultations were humiliating – the way he had made me read aloud from the report, "4mm," at the first meeting to reinforce that my concerns were unfounded (which then turned out to be the wrong size anyway!). Plus the explanation about measuring solid shapes – when he knows I am a teacher and not completely thick!

I then found a website – Braintalk communities. It has a chat room for people with colloid cysts. I read the accounts of other people who have the same concerns that I do. The initial fear and lack of information, the feeling that the medics don't believe our symptoms are real. Everyone has headaches. Everyone suffers some memory loss. Many have dizzy spells or visual disturbances.

There are also accounts from people who have had the cyst removed. They describe the effects of severe hydrocephalus – big confusion, projectile vomiting, agonising pain. I find this reassuring because there is no doubt that I would recognise these symptoms should they occur, I do not have to worry with every severe headache in case it's something serious.

It also gave me the confidence to clarify my thoughts about what I believe about my health, and what I want from the medics. I do think that my cyst is small enough to leave, and that an operation is more risky than its worth while the cyst is small. I do believe that I have symptoms. These are:

I wake most mornings with a headache. It usually fades after about an hour, but sometimes lasts more than a week.

The 'cyst headaches' do not come gradually – they suddenly appear, like my skull has turned to stone, and just as quickly disappear. A 'normal' headache or migraine grows gradually. Also, nothing affects them. When I have a migraine I find light uncomfortable, I want to lie down and pills help the pain to fade. With cyst headaches, nothing seems to make them worse, and pills do not really seem to make them hurt less. It is also less of an ache and more of a pain. The pain is often located at the top of my head.

Sometimes I have a huge pain, like someone has stuck a dagger into the top of my head. It is agony, and can last a few seconds, or a couple of hours. It is big, and sudden, and severe enough to make me drop what I'm carrying or cut myself if I'm peeling vegetables.

When I have headaches I often have a general slowing of thoughts. I can think and speak but it is slow. I need time to process questions and answer them. Sometimes I say the wrong word, can't find names, etc. I can do everything but it requires extra concentration. It is not uncommon for me to say things like, "Right, we need to get ready for ballet. Find your shoes and get in the fridge ready to go."

Something happens to my sight. Things do not blur, nor do I have double vision. But it becomes hard to focus—so sewing would be very difficult but not impossible. Reading is difficult, it's as though the words are moving. I mentioned this to the optician when I had an eye test. He did some tests and said it is the same response as people who have epilepsy but he did not know why.

I 'forget' things. Not just car keys and names—I think everyone my age has trouble with those. But I will not be able to find the light switch in my bedroom and have to look all round for it. When emptying the dishwasher, I will not know where the mugs are kept and will have to open all the cupboards to find them, etc

There are some things which I don't know if they are cyst related or not.

Sometimes I feel I am moving when I am not. Like when you're on a train and the one next to you pulls away and you think your train is moving, then realise that actually you are still in the station. It happens when I am sitting or standing, just for a few seconds, a sort of light headed feeling.

Sometimes the top of my head feels bruised, like a ponytail is too tight but I'm not wearing one.

I have also 'lost time'. I will suddenly realise it is 4 o'clock. My lunch is sitting uneaten on the kitchen table and I cannot account for the time passing. I have been reading, or on the computer—did I just lose track of time or is it more significant than that?

Once, I forgot who my family were, what I was doing, and was totally confused. I think it was due to stress – I was due to go to hospital for a different check up the next day, but I cannot be sure.

That is the frustrating thing with all these symptoms. *All* of them could be entirely due to stress. But I do not for the most part feel stressed (and I have been under significant stress at times in my life so I think I would recognise it).

My belief is that the cyst sometimes slows, though doesn't totally block, the flow of spinal fluid within the brain. This causes intermittent symptoms. I do not know why they seem to be increasing (I have had a headache EVERY morning since November except for 5 days.) Nor do I know if this would leave traces that could be seen on an MRI. I guess if they are something that leaves a trace—and no trace can be seen—then I must be wrong and all this is down to stress or sinuses or something. In that case, they would be curable and I could assume that at some point in the future I could teach or have some other job. (At present I would be much too unreliable as an employee to have a job. I have stopped teaching, and instead I help at a senior's lunch at church, but that's only one day a week. Am a bit useless really.)

I also have learned that a hyper-dense cyst is more easily measured on a CT scan (and in fact sometimes do not show up at all on an MRI) but that due to the risks of radiation it is better to have repeated MRI scans (plus these better show any affects to the brain). I want to check if my understanding of this is correct and also to ask how reliable therefore the MRI measurement of the cyst is. I also read that some people have a 3T MRI. I want to ask if that is what I have and why I need/don't need one.

Therefore, I need to find a medic who will answer my questions. I need someone who will listen to what I am asking and give me straight answers. I do not want him to manage my reactions. If I ask how big the cyst is, I do not want to hear that it is too small to be dangerous; I want to be told the size.

There is a neurosurgeon that some other people in the forum recommend, Mr M. He's at a different hospital, but according to Braintalk Communities, if I ask to be referred to a different consultant, there is not usually a problem. I have therefore asked my doctor to refer me to him. I am now waiting for an appointment. Ideally, I would like to talk with him prior to the MRI, so he can look specifically for signs of intermittent hydrocephalus, if such a thing exists. I hope he will agree that my symptoms are real and will be able to tell me if they are likely to be cyst related.

I need to be convinced of this. I firmly believe they are related, so if they are not I want him to provide me with absolute evidence to the contrary, otherwise I just feel that he somehow does not believe me or that I have explained it inadequately. The fact that I experienced them a few months BEFORE they found the cyst, and that they correspond so closely to other cyst sufferer's symptoms, suggests to me that they are related, and that they are physical and not psychosomatic (which must be a risk once one has read other people's experiences).

Also, any related symptoms are **likely** to be fairly minor if one looks at the available statistics. Most colloid cysts that are under 1cm in size are found incidentally, due to another head trauma, concussion, etc. I believe this is because symptoms tend to be ignored, as either migraine, or are so insignificant they are never reported. This is why colloid cysts have been so dangerous, people with them ignored the symptoms as minor, never got scanned, the cysts were never discovered and people died suddenly as a result. It is only because I know about the cyst that I have analysed them so carefully and can now differentiate between 'normal' headaches and 'cyst' headaches, using the shared experiences of about a hundred other cyst sufferers to hone my evaluations.

I obviously want to know if the cyst is growing. Prior to the last MRI I was confident that it hadn't – almost wondered if it had gone. Now that I have so many headaches I think that maybe it has grown. I am happy to live with it if it is less than 1cm. If it is more than 1cm, I want it removed. I know from reading other people's accounts that throughout the world, most surgeons remove a cyst if it's that size and there is risk of death **even if** it's not symptomatic.

23rd Feb 2010

I had an appointment today with Mr M at NHNN. I had wanted to go on my own but David felt strongly that he wanted to be there so we went together.

Mr M was nice. He is a calm man, who listened carefully and was completely clear in his answers. He looked at my previous MRI and agreed with the previous neurosurgeon's decision. He thought the cyst was probably too small to be causing any symptoms and explained how you can see if hydrocephalus is present.

He explained about CT scans, that cysts are easier to see if they are hyper-dense, plus they give very quick results. However, they also make the cyst 'shine' so the image is not very accurate for measuring, plus the dose of radiation (13 times that given in a chest x-ray) makes them unsuitable for frequent use. Therefore, they are excellent in an emergency when speed is essential but that's about it.

I asked about intermittent hydrocephalus, which I suspect the increased headaches may be due to. He agreed that it would not show up on an MRI unless reasonably severe. However, even slight hydrocephalus would cause traces of 'papilledema', which can be detected by an ophthalmic surgeon. (It is when the optic disc swells, at the point where the optic nerve enters the eyeball, and is associated with an increase in intraocular pressure.)

He therefore suggested that I have another MRI, get my eye test done, and also get a base line neurological behaviour report done—so that any changes can be spotted in the future. I find the last one slightly worrying – how does one give an accurate description of one's behaviour when describing it to a stranger? What if they decide I'm insane?

I said that I assume that even if temporary hydrocephalus is found, given the size of the cyst it can still just be monitored.

He said no, if there is any evidence of symptoms at all, he would be concerned about leaving it. However it seemed clear that he did not think anything would show up on the tests and he was just being thorough. It was a very different experience to consultations with my previous surgeon. I felt listened to, understood, and even though he did not expect the tests to show anything worrying, he was prepared to suggest them, to be certain of his diagnosis. He was not making a decision based on no evidence.

I have the MRI tomorrow and wait to hear for the other tests. I am not sure if then I am just sent the results, or if there will be another consultation.

It has an added hassle involved now, as before they will inject the dye for the MRI, I have to have a blood test to show my kidney function is normal (am guessing that's to ensure the dye is all flushed out afterwards). The MRI team don't do the blood test, I have to ask my GP to do one, and then take the results with me. Asking my GP to do anything is always a hassle (too many patients, too few medics). I did eventually get an appointment to see the nurse, who took blood, and then I was able to collect the results. All hassle. All makes me focus on my health, and not just carry on with life normally.

Not really sure how I feel. I am so SURE that my sudden head pains are caused by the cyst that it is slightly irritating to find that he doesn't think they are. It could just be that my head does not like having a growth in it and so tenses up or something, and causes pain. I am torn between wanting them to find some trace of hydrocephalus so that I have a *reason* for all this pain (which really is beginning to wear me down) and not wanting to have to have an operation that is sure to be awful and possibly life threatening.

I guess that I will have to just wait and see. At least it seems that any decisions about whether to operate will be made by the surgeon so I won't have to agonise about that. I do like this surgeon, he was nice to talk to, so I guess the day's outcome is mainly positive.

Have a headache now. Again. So will write more another time.

6th March 2010

Neuro-psycho thing was fine. Two hours of mental puzzles—tiring, but quite fun. Still waiting for an appointment from opthalmologist. Will email and ask for his phone number to try and hurry things up a bit.

Still getting daily headaches. Dreary. No idea if cyst related or stress. I wake at 4.30 every morning with the pain, so tired too.

8th March

David emailed Mr M's secretary for me, so now I have number for opthalmologist. Trying to make appointment. It's horrid waiting, I can't just forget about it and get on with life.

15th March

Finally got appointment—for next Wednesday. Feel much better just knowing it's in the diary.

24th March

Went to Moorfields, the eye hospital. It was busy, and I had to wait ages. There was no way of knowing how soon you would be called, so I daren't go to the loo or to get a coffee, in case they called my name and I missed my appointment. My head hurt (of course) so it was all very uncomfortable.

The opthalmologist was nice, and seemed intelligent. He tested a few things—like my peripheral vision (I had to stick my head in a machine and press a button whenever I saw dots light up). He also took a photo of the back of my eye. He put some drops into my eyes, which did something to my pupils, so I couldn't see. The world was fuzzy. I was then taken to a different department for the photo, and had to be led there by a porter, which was very weird.

After the photo, I was told I could go home—but I still couldn't see anything. I managed to hail a taxi, and he took me to the station. Finding the right platform was difficult, I had to listen for announcements and ask people. If there had been a hole in the ground, I would've walked into it—I really could see very little. I couldn't even see to text or phone David for help. I didn't know when the drops would wear off. I managed to get the right train, but when I arrived in Oxted, I still couldn't see well enough to drive home. I'd parked in a 3 hour limit parking space, so I waited with the car, and when a traffic warden came, I explained that I couldn't see and was waiting for my daughter to drive me home. Then I sat in Cafe Nero until the school bus arrived.

Eventually the drops wore off, and my eyes just felt heavy, but I could see. I cannot believe the hospital didn't warn me that I wouldn't be able to drive afterwards!

30th March 2010

Went to see Mr M for test results. I thought the appointment was 1.30 (I am SURE that's the time his secretary said, and wrote it in my diary). But when I arrived, they said it was at 11.30, and I'd missed it. I cried. (Embarrassing)

They phoned Mr M, and he told me to get a taxi to the Wellington, and he'd see me there. Very kind of him. They gave me my file to carry (there was a lot of paper in there!)

Mr M said although the ventricles were slightly enlarged, there was no need to do anything yet, and he would continue to monitor me. The neuropsychology test was fine (and actually, I am more intelligent than suspected—will need to remind family of this regularly). Also, the ophthalmologist had found no distortion of the optic disc, but also there was no pulse in the vein (which I think there should be). So, he said that whilst he didn't think there was anything to worry about, he thought it was sensible to re-do the three tests in six months. Ugh.

The tests were repeated in September, but I obviously decided there was nothing worth writing in my diary, as I didn't mention them. As they showed little change,

30

Mr. M asked me to repeat them after another 12 months

November 2010

Mr M referred me to a neurologist to help control the headaches. I went to see Mr L.

I explained about the increase in headaches, that they tend to come in clusters and that they often feel like a 'bruising' on the inside of my skull. He listened, asked sensible questions and was prepared to discuss options. He examined my head but could not feel anything unusual. He thinks that the headaches are migraines and not related to the cyst. (Heard that one before.)

I asked whether it was possible that the cyst was *causing* migraines, as there are no obvious triggers. He agreed it was possible. I decided I do not care WHAT is causing the headaches, I just want them to stop. He prescribed triptans.

May 2011

Nothing has changed. Mr L has suggested I try mild anti-depressants to try and prevent the migraines. I will try them and see what happens.

12th September 2012

At my last appointment with Mr M, he said the MRI showed there was no change in size or position to the previous one. However, he said his team had reviewed my first and second MRIs and they felt that some of the ventricles had enlarged during that time.

I am now in the process of repeating the tests. The hardest bit was probably making the appointments. His secretary was a student temp, who after two weeks hadn't contacted me with any appointments, or got the MRI referral. I hassled him for the MRI email to be sent and then phoned the other places directly (not easy as all the extension numbers were wrong).

I eventually had the MRI last week. I hate when they wedge my head still, and it's so hard to go into the machine and keep my eyes shut so I can't see how enclosed I am, but it happened and is done. It actually feels harder doing all these medical tests now. I guess all the adrenaline is gone, they are horrible and a hassle, and life is dreary.

Tomorrow is the neuropsychology assessment and the eye chap is in a couple of weeks. I see Mr M on 12th Oct for the results – I decided not to cancel everything for his first available appointment, as I am assuming all will be the same. Also assume if anything urgent shows up he would contact me. (This is a good sign, it shows I am becoming more rational about all this health stuff. It is becoming 'normal').

Headaches continue. I don't think they are any worse (though David does). They still come in clusters. They're rarely so bad that I can't function, though at a much slower pace and feeling pretty fed up. I do need to try and get some different pills. I take a lot of Excedrin (which I can buy over the counter in the US) and I'm not sure that so much aspirin is good for me.

I am still no longer working. I was too unreliable to be the teacher I wanted to be, and also worried that if I 'got in a muddle' when caring for children it could be dangerous.

Instead, I am learning Mandarin. The lessons were offered to parents by Will's school, and it seemed a good opportunity to 'do' something. They have turned out to be excellent therapy. The lessons completely absorb my thoughts, which gives me a complete break from worry for one hour a week. I also have lots of opportunity to practice in hospital waiting rooms. I have found it is impossible to 'not think'. Instead, I am filling my thoughts with things unrelated to my health.

Mandarin is quite difficult, I have to concentrate on new words completely. I have bought some DVDs, and when I have a bad head and am unable to do anything else, I can listen to it playing and try to absorb some of the tones and words. It helps me to feel less useless, less like an afternoon spent lying in a dark room is a complete waste of life.

14th September 2012

Completely fed up. I am going for these tests, neuropsychology was yesterday. It's not completely unpleasant, is vaguely interesting and gets me out of the house. But I am sure nothing will change. Mr M will tell me that everything is stable and static and to check in a few months time but that is all. I am so TIRED of having headaches. I don't feel like doing anything, they sap my enthusiasm. True, I am rarely in bed with them, but they get in the way, they make even simple things a chore. I have had enough now.

When I talk about my "brain tumour" I feel like a fraud. It isn't life threatening, they wont operate, it isn't big. But it is always with me. I try to forget it, but it is in my thoughts every single day. Whenever something unusual happens (like, I keep getting black spots in my eyes and my ears keep 'popping' like after a flight – more likely to be due to a cold germ than the cyst) I wonder if it's related to the cyst. Nothing is normal anymore. I am not Anne, I am Anne with a thing in my brain.

I sort of hope it will explode. Then I will clearly be ill, there will be a clear treatment, and I can get completely better. Today is another headache day. About two weeks in a row now. Not bad ones, just there, an ache that distracts. Intensely fed up.

The anti-depressants did nothing other than give me nightmares and make me sleepy, so I stopped taking them. If I have a really bad pain, I take triptans. Mr. L has prescribed them in injection form, as he thought my stomach was shutting down due to the pain, so I wasn't absorbing the pills. At least now, if I need to do something, I know I can give myself an injection to get rid of the pain. They usually work (though I can feel the blood moving in my hands when I do them, which is very odd). The first time was rather scary. It is like an epi pen, that we used at school for children with allergies. I simply stab it into my leg and it works almost instantly. Or not at all—seems to depend on headache.

19th September 2012

Still fed up, still have some head pain most of the time. Not sure if I am getting used to it, so it doesn't stop me functioning (all be it at a slower pace) or if I have just become so 'head focused' that even the slightest twinge – which everyone else would ignore – is very noticeable.

Most of the time it feels almost like bruising on top of my head. Not sure how long it has felt like that (almost like a hair band is too tight, even though I don't ever wear one). I have also noticed a sort of 'fizzing' in my head. If I rotate my head I can feel a sort of grinding/fizzing sensation across the back of my head. Does the brain have air in it? Could I have air bubbles in there? And if so, could that be the cause of my headaches rather than the cyst? I want to stop thinking about it now. But every time I get another twinge it reminds me.

Mr L, the new neurologist, has actually been very helpful. He explained to me that my increased headaches are, in his opinion, migraines, but they might be being triggered by the cyst—he is unable to say for sure because there's no evidence. It seems that everything medics say has to be based on evidence. So, the neurosurgeons said the cyst is not symptomatic—not because they don't believe I am in pain, but because there is *no evidence of what is causing the pain.* If there was physiological evidence, they would say it was symptomatic.

I looked at what defines a migraine online. It is rather more than I had realised. The trouble with speech (aphasia) is a common part of migraine. So is the complete lack of energy following an attack. The fact that triptans sometimes work is also a sign that I am having migraines, at least some of the time.

I still think I have intermittent hydrocephalus. At my last ophthalmologist's appointment, he said that papilledema would only show up if there was severe and sustained (more than 24 hours) pressure in the brain. It is therefore, completely possible that the cyst causes some build-up of cerebrospinal fluid, but not enough to leave any visible sign. I think this intermittent hydrocephalus triggers migraines. But I can't prove that, and even if I could, it wouldn't change anything. I am still better off NOT having the surgery—which I understand almost always causes headaches afterwards, and often is dangerous. I do not want to die, or lose my memory, or speech, or ability to think. I can cope with headaches. It's rather draining though….

September 2013

There is still no change. The headaches come in clusters, I will have several months with no pain at all, then headaches for six weeks. They are unrelated to hormones, stressful events, foods and anything else that I can monitor. They are not usually severe enough to stop me functioning, and when they are bad they tend to be migraines and I can take triptans.

Occasionally I have a really bad headache, one where I feel like the pain will drive me crazy and of course, added to this is always the worry that this is IT, the unusual *big headache* which is meant to send me running to the hospital for a CT scan. But how big is big? How painful is painful? They hurt, and sometimes they hurt so much I pull at my hair, just so I can feel a different sort of pain. But so far, none have been fatal. Usually, the triptan injection makes them stop (sounds like something out of Star Trek!) But sometimes, nothing works and I feel quite desperate until finally, hours later, they fade.

I am still having regular MRI, though now phone for the results rather than travelling up to London. I asked Mr M if he could text the results—he could send a: *"No Change"* or: *"Don't start any long books"* message. He laughed, and said I could phone in. It helps to keep things in perspective if I spend less time doing health related things.

The long lasting 'top of the head' headaches are not affected by anything. Nothing makes them worse (except perhaps lying down) so I can cycle, cook, shop, and so on, but just feel awful. They take the edge off life—I still enjoy things, but usually through a fuzz of discomfort.

I rarely think about the cyst now. My life is full of voluntary work (which I can cancel at the last minute if I have a headache) and teaching English in the local Chinese restaurants (my Mandarin is now fairly fluent). I have had to build a life full of things that don't matter if I cancel them, because I can't predict when I'll have a headache that's too bad for me to drive safely. It's actually a good life, I am doing enough to feel useful—I guess everyone wants to know there's a purpose to their life.

I have come to believe that my cyst will never change and it is just something I will live with. In some ways it makes me live a better life because I am very aware that I am potentially very temporary. Most people my age have something unpleasant, bad backs or depression seem to me to be much more debilitating than headaches.

Perhaps, I am actually living a better life. When you know you might die tomorrow, you live today very carefully.

The last time I talked about the cyst to my GP (a new one, Dr B retired) she said, "It sounds like you think you might die!" I was there about something else, a routine check-up, but she had mentioned the cyst, so I'd told her that I never noticed anything I thought was dangerous.

"Well," I said, feeling embarrassed, "every consultation I have had finishes with a list of symptoms, any of which they tell me, should send me straight to hospital—just in case the cyst has changed."

"Oh," she said, "they are just covering themselves!"

I believed her.

Chapter Two
Living with a Colloid Cyst : What I learned

There is more to my story, but first I thought it might be helpful to tell you what I learned while I had the colloid cyst. Because actually, I learned a lot. If you, or someone close to you, is diagnosed with a brain tumour, I hope something here might be useful.

Community Helps — Usually

When you are first diagnosed with any type of brain tumour (and I am guessing any kind of cancer is the same) it is very scary. With a brain tumour, I also felt very isolated—I had never even met anyone who had undergone brain surgery. Finding the Braintalk Community website was brilliant. There are now several Facebook groups which are similar, and to read other people's experiences, and be able to ask questions, is invaluable. I would definitely suggest you should try to find a group with your particular tumour. (If you can't find one, start one.)

I do think this is especially important for young people. I have listened to several teenagers, who describe how they miss so much school that all their friends, who were hugely supportive initially, sort of 'move on' and they feel excluded. Add to that the peers they see most often are the other patients in hospital, many of whom die, and it makes for a very lonely life. Coping with a brain tumour is horrid enough as it is, being a teenager is also pretty hard—having to cope with both is awful. But being with people in a similar position, finding friends who understand, can help a lot.

However, you do need to be aware that the people in the group are just that—people. They may have their own issues and needs, and some of the comments might not be helpful. Some people are lonely, or suffering with depression, and their comments may not reflect reality. So do be wise when reading, and careful about what you write.

There is also the community you mix in each day. What you choose to tell people is your own decision. I wanted my family to trust I was being honest with them, so I told them everything, but in as un-frightening a way as possible. So I told my children (then all teenagers) that the colloid cyst was like a bubble in my brain, and we tended to refer to it as Bubble.

Some people will make up their own minds about what is wrong with you. I found some people behaved as if I was an invalid, others expected me to continue as usual, with no idea that I was struggling with almost constant pain. Brain tumours cannot be seen, nor can headaches, double vision, attention deficit, and all the other lovely effects that we live with. If we had a broken leg, everyone would know we probably shouldn't be walking up a mountain. With a brain tumour, it's up to us to tell people what we find difficult, and to be clear about our abilities.

However, we also need to be careful not to use the brain tumour as an excuse. It was easy for me to opt out of things I didn't *want to do* by saying I had a brain tumour, when sometimes, I could have coped just fine. I remember chatting about this one day to a friend, who has had multiple strokes and walks with a stick. She admitted that sometimes she tells people she cannot go to events, or help with something, because of her disability, when actually, she simply didn't want to. I guess it's something everyone with a disability is tempted to do. But I'm not sure it's good for us. Don't let having a brain tumour define you—it is not who you are.

You are still you. Even if you have to modify your life, there is still lots you can do, you still have something to offer. If you can no longer manage paid employment, find something voluntary you can work at. Being useful, needed, is hugely important. Sometimes after diagnosis, people turn into a 'patient' and that's all. But everyone has something to give, even if it's taking cookies to share with the nurses at an appointment, offering to do a flower arrangement at church, putting away the returned books in the library, setting the table at a lunch club for seniors. Find a role, something where you can help, and do it whenever your health allows. And do it well. As time goes on, if your condition worsens, you may have to adapt or reduce what you give to others. But don't stop altogether. You still have a role.

Neurosurgeons

One of the main things I learned about neurosurgeons, and it took a while, is that they are human too. I was under two very different neurosurgeons—one who I clashed with, and one who was very helpful and who treated me like his equal. It *is* possible to find a surgeon who will listen to you and explain things properly, but you might have to search for one.

It sounds obvious, but actually, it helps if we understand what they're thinking when they say things, so we don't misinterpret their words. We expect our surgeon to be great at the chopping bit, and great at the communication bit. But many are not so good at communicating, and sometimes what they *say* is not what they *mean*. So, when they told me my colloid cyst was not symptomatic, it didn't mean they didn't believe I was in pain. It meant they couldn't find a physiological reason for the pain. Because colloid cysts are rare, and they knew very little about them.

Actually, the understanding of colloid cysts is already changing, and the more recent articles *do* say that they cause migraines and headaches (everything I read in 2009 said they did not unless there was hydrocephalus). The thing is, neurosurgery is relatively new.

Historians know that early man *did* perform brain surgery —possibly to treat conditions thought to be demon possession (which were probably epilepsy)—because they have found remains of skulls that have been neatly drilled into. The patients probably all died (well, they were 'early man', so of course they died, or they would be centuries old now. But I mean, they probably died due to the surgery. Obviously.)

However, for the longest time, well after surgeons were operating on hearts and kidneys and limbs, most did not venture into the skull. The skull is an enclosed space, which they thought was best left intact. So brain surgery is a bit behind all the other medical fields. It is catching up—and catching up fast. When I was diagnosed in 2009, the method of removing colloid cysts was different to how it was in 2014. Brain surgery is getting better every year, the chances of surviving brain surgery without major damage is also improving. So, if you are looking for information online (which I do not recommend, but we all do it) then take careful note of the dates on the articles you read. A paper written ten years ago might be wrong.

Then there is the personality of the surgeons themselves. I have friends who are medics (actually, at 52, my *children* have friends who are medics—which is a very scary thought!). But anyway, I have spoken to friends who are surgeons, though

41

none of them are brain surgeons. The thing is, brain surgery is not intrinsically more difficult than other surgery—but the odds are bigger. If you make a mistake with other surgery, usually, it can be put right. But brains aren't like that. One tiny error can be fatal. Literally.

So the people who sign up for that kind of pressure have to, in my opinion, be a special kind of person. A sort of dare-devil, or super confident individual. Someone who is brave enough to put their knowledge into practice, and live with the consequences. That does not necessarily make for a personality who is a good listener. Or one who takes into account what others (the patient) wants. Some do—I was fortunate enough to find a neurosurgeon who was both an excellent surgeon AND a good consultant/listener. But I suspect they are rare. At the end of the day, do you care more about being listened to, or more about having someone who's brilliant in the operating room? You might have to choose.

Now, I thought, when I was first diagnosed, that I had to stay with the first surgeon I was referred to. As you will have read in my diary, I didn't much like my first surgeon. I didn't trust him to answer my questions honestly, and felt 'managed' by him. Switching was so easy. If you're unhappy, try to find the name of someone recommended by other people with your condition, go to your GP, and ask to be referred to them instead. It happens all the time, there's nothing personal about it. Do it.

Also, do remember that you do not have to wait to be sent an appointment. When your GP has referred you to a specialist, ask for their contact details. You can then phone them, explain you have been referred, and make an appointment. It saves a lot of time.

Living with the Stress

Okay, so whether they operate or not, you will probably be rather stressed. Here are a few suggestions that might help:

Occupy your mind. I found that I could not stop thinking about the fact that I had a brain tumour and was in danger of it defining who I was. It is impossible to 'not think' about something, so filling your mind with something else is a huge help.

I started to learn Mandarin after being diagnosed, and this was wonderful. I am not a linguist, cannot speak any other language at all, and gave my language teachers at school nervous breakdowns! However, Mandarin was fabulous. It is fairly difficult, so I concentrated with my whole mind during lessons and there was no time to worry about anything else. It was a great distraction in all those boring hospital waiting rooms. Obviously a language might not be your 'thing', but I really would suggest that you find some hobby to occupy your mind, to give it a break from worrying. Whether it is chess, knitting or kick-boxing, find something that is quite difficult, fits into your schedule and that you enjoy.

Secondly, do some exercise. Whether they operate or not, you want a healthy body. Cycling as fast as you can or swimming a few laps, is another good way to burn off some stress and give yourself a break. Even if you are too weak for anything else, go for a walk. I had lots of pretty bad headaches, but I found that cycling did not make them any worse, and I felt better in myself after I had exercised. You should check with your doctor that you are safe to exercise, but if there is no reason not to, I would say force yourself to.

Thirdly, be nice to yourself. If it was a close friend suffering, you would give them treats, encourage them to do

43

things they enjoy, etc. Do the same for yourself. You are special, going through a tough time, allow yourself some treats.

Try not to face things you do not need to. Sometimes our thoughts run away with us and we imagine being handicapped, mute, dependent and so on, when actually these things are unlikely to happen today. Try to live in the present, each day face what has to be faced that day. Don't worry about the future until you have to. (You could still get run over by a bus, then all that worry will have been for nothing!)

Pray. If you have sorted out what you believe, now is the time to put it to the test. It's not worth having faith in something that cannot help you right now. Praying is not a 'genie in a lamp', it changes us over time but I do believe that it helps hugely. If you decide that you do not believe in any God at all, then I don't know what to suggest (maybe re-think..?)

Death

Any growth in the brain is likely to be nasty. True, some sit there quite happily and never cause any problems, but the vast majority are bad news. If you have a brain tumour, you need to recognise that they're dangerous. So are motorbikes, being very drunk, and eating food from a student's fridge. The point is, EVERYONE has a 'use-by' date. We will all die at some point, but most people, most of the time, can ignore that. If you have a brain tumour, it's kind of thrown in your face in an I-can't-ignore-this way. Which can be very frightening.

I found that very few people ever mentioned dying to me. Except for the medics, who were very honest about the fact that the colloid cyst might prove fatal. However, I think, personally, that this is an issue that needs to be faced. If you have a brain tumour, you know, deep down, that it might kill you. If you ignore that, never sort out what your beliefs are, then I think those thoughts can fester in an unhealthy way.

My advice is : sort out what you believe about death. I am a Christian, but actually, the fear of dying, leaving my children, missing what comes next, was very frightening. I absolutely did not want to die. I still don't. But when I prayed that through, thought about what I really believed, it helped. If dying was the worst thing that could happen, and I sorted out that, then a lot of the stress was eased.

So, what do you believe? Most people follow the religion they were brought up in, even if they've never really thought it through for themselves. Now is the time to think about it. Medical knowledge has improved amazingly, having a brain tumour may not kill you. But it might, so be a grown up and sort out your beliefs.

If you know that your tumour is *likely* to be fatal, then you need to decide how you want to cope with that. I have never died (obviously) but my Dad has, so I will tell you a little of his story, because it might help.

Dad had prostate cancer, which went fairly quickly into his bones. Every time he went for a medical check-up, the cancer had progressed—at first slowly, then fairly quickly. At first he was told "prostate cancer is something you die *with*, not *from*, it is rarely fatal." Then the cancer went into his bones. Not much later, he was told the cancer was in his liver, and there was nothing more they could do. Now, we are a close family, and my dad was good at sharing, expressing his feelings, so I learnt a lot from him. In fact, I feel that in those final months, Dad taught me how to die. He died a good death.

At first, the discomfort of the cancer was all Dad talked about. He couldn't sleep, he had no appetite, the chemo left him exhausted (and strangely, all he fancied eating was gammon—my mum had to cook a lot of gammon in those days!) Cancer in bones is extremely painful.

He decided he did not want to know his prognosis. He said—once he knew that there was no hope the medics could cure him—that he didn't want to know how long they expected him to live for. He thought it would make him constantly aware of having 'three weeks left', knowing he wouldn't attend events a year from now, and so on. He gave permission for us, as a family, to find out the prognosis, so we knew he was likely to live for another three months, but he chose not to know.

For the family, it was hugely important that we knew—so my sister in Canada could be told to come and visit, so we could start making sensible decisions. But Dad didn't want to know. In many ways, this made it very hard for the rest of us, because he delayed doing things he needed to do (like making a will). However, I do understand his logic. Now, I'm not sure what I think about that, but you should consider what you want. It is your choice.

Of course, Dad wasn't stupid, he knew he was dying. He simply chose to not know the date. As he grew weaker, as the cancer caused him constant pain, ate away his flesh, stole his hair, Dad changed. He began to read the Bible with fresh eyes, he grew excited about things he discovered about God. I felt, as an onlooker, that I was watching him become gradually less physical, and ever more spiritual. For Dad, he clung onto God, and God did not let him down.

People did though. Dad was no saint, and he was often irritated by the nurses who visited, or the people at church who he hardly knew that wanted to gush over him and pray prayers on his behalf. I remember him choosing to not attend an event at church, because he knew his appearance (a kind of 'nearly dead' look) would upset other people.

"I can cope with dying myself," he said, "but I can't cope with other people's reactions."

I do understand what he meant, because when I was diagnosed with the tumour, it was carrying other people's worries that was the hardest. Sometimes we need to protect ourselves from what others, those close to us, are saying and feeling. They need to be able to let off steam, have their say, let out their emotions—*but not with the patient!* If people are sharing too much of their own grief, it is okay for you to ask them to tell someone else. In fact, if your tumour is likely to be terminal, it is kindest if you gradually move away from being their emotional support, and force them to find other help. Then afterwards, when you have left them, they will be used to going to others for comfort.

One final thought about Dad—he never gave up. He died the 1st January, and the Boxing Day before, we had a big party with all the extended family at my uncle's house. I remember my dad, sitting in a chair before we went, shaving and applying aftershave. He was very weak, and all his movements were very slow. He saw me watching, and smiled.

"I'm not giving up, Annie," he said.

The following day, just a couple of days before he died, he told my mum he'd had "the best Christmas I've ever had." Which says everything really. Whatever is coming, however long we have, until we're dead we're alive, and able to enjoy the life we have. Don't let anyone take that away from you.

Brains

I guess every person with a brain tumour learns something about brains, even if it's only the very basics. This is what I learned (which isn't much, but may help if you have been recently diagnosed). Please remember that I have written a hugely simplified explanation, which would probably make a medic shudder—but hopefully it will be useful.

Messages travel between the left and right of the brain, and between them are ventricles. Ventricles are basically just drains, where all the spinal fluid flows. Ventricles are significant if you have a colloid cyst, because they tend to be found in the third ventricle, right in the middle of the brain. If they are tiny, like a little grape on a stem, they can sit there undetected, not causing any harm. If they move (like the grape swaying on the stem) or if they grow, they can block the flow of spinal fluid. Spinal fluid carries messages from the brain to the body—it tells the heart to beat, the lungs to breathe. If the fluid is suddenly stopped, because an undetected cyst has grown big enough to completely block the ventricle, everything stops. Hence the 'sudden instant death'.

However, my understanding is that usually, they cause problems before this—they stop some of the flow, causing a build up of fluid in the brain, or hydrocephalus. This extra fluid stops the brain functioning as it should, the pressure causes headaches, feeling fuzzy, dizzy spells. It can press on the optic nerve, stretching it, so the person becomes very short-sighted, or has double vision.

The brain has two main halves—the left and the right. They do different things, and I actually found it helpful to imagine the brain being in different sections, each one with a different function. It is way more complicated than that, but unless you plan to be a surgeon, it's probably all you need to know.

The left side of the brain controls your language. All your language. So your speaking, your thinking in words, your ability to read, to understand what someone is saying to you —that is all in the left side of your brain. It is how we make sense of the world, so when you see a tree, and think: "tree" that is the left side of your brain.

I learned about this when I was studying to be a teacher, because sometimes students need to learn to use a particular side of their brain. When you are drawing, if you look at a face and draw an 'eye', it probably won't be a very good likeness. If however, you force yourself to use the right side of your brain, and instead of drawing 'an eye' you draw curves of certain lengths, at certain distances, noticing the spaces between them—probably your picture of an 'eye' will be more accurate.

This means that generally, if the left side of a brain is damaged—through surgery or a stroke, then a person's speech will be affected. All their speech—so giving a relative who can't speak an iPad to type on, will not help their communication. The brain *can* repair, will find new ways around the damaged area, and people often regain their language, but it can take time.

As an aside, I learned more about this while researching what defines a psychopath, when writing a novel. Apparently, it is thought that psychopaths are unusual, in having a second speech centre in the right side of the brain, which is why they often speak in muddled ways—are said to talk in 'word salad' and will sometimes contradict themselves within a single sentence. So, for example, they might say: "I am never violent, I would only kill if someone annoyed me". This is completely irrelevant to brain tumours, but is quite interesting, don't you think?

It is because speech is located in the left side of the brain, that when colloid cysts were removed in the past, and the surgeon cut across the top of the head, from ear to ear, that sometimes people were left mute. If at all possible, surgeons now avoid damaging the left side of the brain.

The left side of the brain controls:

the right side of the body (your right arm, right hand, etc)
analytical thought
speech
logic
science and maths
practical issues
verbal memory (what you have heard or read)

The right side of the brain controls:
holistic thought
the left side of your body
intuition
creativity
art and music
feeling, imagination
spatial awareness
risk taking
rhythm
problem awareness
visual memory (what you have seen)

So, very simply put, the left side of your brain knows an object is a fork, the right side of your brain knows how to use it.

The back of your brain is concerned with your vision (so if someone thumps you on the back of your head, you might see stars).

The top of your brain controls movement (so a bang on top of your head might make you fall on the floor).

The front part of your brain controls planning, motivation, multi-tasking, sequencing, and controls emotions (and emotion based behaviour).

In the past, when they tried to change the behaviour of violent patients by doing a frontal lobotomy, they found that although it did stop people being violent, it also stopped them being motivated. (I think they removed the frontal lobe, because it was dysfunctional.) The resultant complete lack of motivation meant they would stop doing everything, and just sat, staring into space.

I also discovered (with my book research) that psychopaths are born with an under-developed frontal lobe, which might explain why they are unable to have emotional empathy, and why they do not control their emotional impulses. It is the frontal lobe that stops you hitting the annoying lady in the post-office queue...

*

Following the removal of a colloid cyst, many people complain about memory loss. There seem to be three types of memory: immediate memory (you can repeat a sequence you have just been told); short term memory (you can recall information after about half an hour); long term memory (you remember things from more than a day ago). Most people with colloid cysts seem to complain about memory loss, and it seems to be worse after surgery, due to the brain being damaged.

Two things I found helpful, were knowing that memory is affected by both *tiredness* and *stress*.

So, if you have a brain tumour, you are probably stressed about it, and your memory issues might be due to that rather than the tumour itself. Also, if you are planning a stressful event—such as visiting a neurosurgeon—it is worth taking someone else with you, as you are likely to forget what you want to ask, and what the surgeon says to you. Or take a list with you, and write down what you're told. It is very annoying when you get back home and realise you forgot to mention half your worries, and you have absolutely no idea what he said to you during the meeting. I used to take my husband (I did ban him from speaking during the visit, so I still felt in control) and it was surprising afterwards how his memory of the consultation was so very different to mine.

Following surgery, the brain gets very tired. All those clever electric messages are having to find new routes around the brain, they can't just buzz from the left to the right anymore, they have to go via a new way to avoid the scar caused by surgery. This is exhausting. When we are exhausted, we forget things. So, if you need to remember things, learn them in the morning, when you'll be less tired. This is a shame if you're a 'study all night before the exam' kind of person, but you won't remember things learnt at the last minute, when tired. You might have to become one of those well prepared students who studies in the mornings.

If someone tells you something while you're busy working on something else, ask them to write it down for you—or stop and send yourself a text. Knowing our short term memory is pretty useless is not an excuse for not finding solutions.

Migraines

When I was first diagnosed with the colloid cyst, everyone told me the headaches I was having were migraines, and unrelated to the cyst. I found this extremely frustrating, as I was sure they were different to the migraines I had been having since childhood.

However, some of my frustration was because I didn't, actually, understand *what* a migraine was. To me, it was a 'sick headache'. When I eventually saw Mr L the neurologist, he explained exactly what a migraine might look like. It was surprisingly like the headaches I was having! My own view now, is that the cyst was causing migraines. So, what IS a migraine?

There is a lot of information online, so I suggest you look there for more details, but here is my own, layperson's brief summary:

A migraine is caused by messed up electrical activity in the brain. (It is actually to do with brain ion homeostasis—which is potassium leaking out of the cells, and sodium and calcium filling the gaps—which is called CSD. The capillaries to the brain first have too much blood, which can cause an aura. The body reacts to this by constricting the flow, which is when the pain hits. So some migraine medicines, like triptans, work by altering the flow of blood to the brain. But that is way too complicated for this summary.)

Basically, it's usually a headache with some sensory disturbances thrown in for added interest. A 'sensory disturbance' includes things like increased sensitivity to light (so you want the curtains closed) or smells (in my case, I can tell what people ate for their last meal and who my husband has been sitting next to at work, just from the smell).

There are two main types of migraine—those with aura, and those without. The most common are migraines without aura (about 80% of migraines don't have aura).

A migraine *without aura* is also called a 'common migraine' (so you don't want to have one of those—who wants to be common?) The symptoms are a throbbing pain, usually on one side of the head (in fact, the Mandarin translation of 'migraine' is 'one-sided headache'), sickness and diarrhoea (not always, sometimes you just feel sick) and sensitivity to light.

A migraine *with aura* has all the above symptoms, plus visual disturbances. For me, this means I suddenly have a blind spot, so my vision has a gap—like looking through a window with a misty circle in the corner. (It's annoying, as if I'm driving it means I have to stop, and wait for it to pass.) Some people see zigzag lines, or coloured spots, or even have temporary blindness. Some people have numbness or tingles, or pins and needles in their limbs. Some people have vertigo (dizziness). Some people experience memory loss (once, when I was teaching, I suddenly realised I couldn't remember the names of my pupils. None of them. It was very frightening.) Some people find their speech is affected (like my substituting words) or their hearing. Some people have weakness in one side of their body.

A migraine with brainstem aura means there might be loss of balance, double vision, and fainting.

Familial hemiplegic migraine means people suffer temporary paralysis (which must be extremely scary the first time that happens).

So you see, there is more to a migraine than 'just' a headache. Many of the people who contribute to the Facebook groups I follow, despair that their neurosurgeon has told them they "just have migraines", which they are sure is incorrect. They then go on to list many of the above symptoms (hence suggesting that they *do* have migraines—which might be, in my opinion, being triggered by the cyst). I think the problem is often not in diagnosis, but in telling us, the patient, exactly what is meant by the diagnosis.

A migraine can last from 4 to 72 hours. If you have a migraine for more than 15 days in each month, you are said to have chronic migraine. Neurologists are often able to help with the pain. Mine prescribed triptans, and they did help (though by the end, I was having almost constant migraines, and there is a limit to how often you should take triptans, so you have to be careful).

Before a migraine, you may begin to have symptoms, like the aura, or a craving for sweet food, or needing to sleep. After a migraine, you feel exhausted, a sort of 'migraine hangover'. So, there are actually three stages to a migraine.

There are also migraines with *no* pain—which I was told are called 'silent migraines'. You might have the aura—perhaps zigzag flashes, and feel slightly fuzzy, but never actually have the headache.

Some people who have migraines also have what are known as "ice pick" headaches, or idiopathic stabbing headaches. These feel like someone has stuck an ice pick into your head. They are sudden, violent pains, which usually disappear as quickly as they arrive.

Neuroscientists think that migraines tend to run in families, and are set off by certain triggers. Different people have different triggers, and I have read that you need at least two triggers to get a migraine. So if you can detect what triggers your own migraines, you might be able to prevent them. Keeping a diary of your headaches might help with this

—or it might make you focus so much on your health that you can't ever forget it, in which case you're better off just guessing (in my opinion). Here are the triggers which are most commonly listed:

Change in your routine. (My dad always had migraines at the weekend.)

Stress (or the release of stress).

Change in the amount of sleep (so either too much, or too little).

Hormones (women and teenagers will relate to this one).

Too much caffeine (or a sudden drop in amount of caffeine—so cut down slowly).

High altitude, humidity, or weather changes. (I know someone who always gets a migraine right before a thunder storm.)

Computer screens (so don't spend too long working/playing games).

Food changes (as in, missing a meal).

Red wine (because it contains tyramine; so do Brie and Camembert, so they can be triggers too).

Dehydration.

Cocaine and cannabis (perhaps you shouldn't be taking those anyway….)

Unusual exercise (either a sudden increase or decrease).

Head injury.

Muscle tension (as in, tense muscles in your neck)

I will also add brain tumour/colloid cysts. This has never, as far as I know, been proven, but it seems flaming obvious to me after hearing from so many colloid cyst sufferers, and from my own experience.

Some people think that chocolate is also a trigger. However, I will not include that. Partly because neuroscientists think the reason for this is because the early stage of migraine tends to prompt a craving for sweet food— so people eat chocolate. Then they get a migraine and think the chocolate *caused* it, whereas actually it was merely a symptom. Mainly, I am not including it because life without chocolate would be way too depressing.

Now, the above list shows something of the difficulty that arises with some brain tumours. The symptoms of migraine can be very similar to those of a brain tumour—so is it possible to define the cause? Obviously sometimes it is—if for example, there is clear evidence of hydrocephalus on a scan, then a patient suffering from dizzy spells and feeling sick and head pain can be told that this is due to their tumour. But if there is no visible evidence, if the hydrocephalus is intermittent, then the issue becomes more complicated.

My understanding is that migraines last up to 72 hours, and after that, there will be no symptoms at all. So, if a patient does not feel dizzy always, every day, then it might be concluded that the dizziness is due to migraine, not the tumour.

However, for colloid cyst sufferers, the problem is that slight hydrocephalus itself might be intermittent, which means the symptoms of the cyst/hydrocephalus are also intermittent. This is because a very small cyst can move, due to being on a sort of stalk. Unless one has an MRI every day (and I think they cost about £1,000 each, so that's never going to happen) there is, I guess, no way of knowing. I should note that these are my own observations and conclusions, you might want to check with your neurosurgeon.

However, does it matter? I decided, after dragging myself through life with almost constant migraines, that actually, I didn't care *what* the medics said was causing the pain, I just wanted it to stop. If there was migraine relief that would help, then fine. The hydrocephalus could not be extreme, because it wasn't affecting what could be seen when a doctor examined behind my eyes, therefore it couldn't be dangerous. Although I would (before I knew better) have chosen to have the cyst removed just so the pain could be stopped. I later learned that actually, brain surgery itself usually causes head pain. One surgeon I spoke to told me that in most cases, patients have severe head pains following surgery, and they're not completely sure why. So removing the cyst could cause a whole new lot of problems.

My advice is this: if you are told the pain is not linked to the colloid cyst, and your symptoms match those I have mentioned above, then it is safe to assume they might be due to migraine. There might be medicine, designed to alleviate migraine, which can help you. If the pain becomes worse, or if your vision starts to get worse, then go to hospital. This is not an easy task—to know when the headache has 'changed'. If you have constant pain, it is actually very hard to know if it's worse than the day before, or different in any way. I think, if in doubt, go to hospital. You may have a couple of 'false alarms' —I certainly did, and twice presented myself at A&E asking to be checked when it wasn't necessary. But gradually you will learn what is 'normal' and stop being anxious. It is better to be safe than sorry.

MRI Machines (Or, Magnetic Resonance Imaging)

The main thing I learnt about MRI machines is that they are different. All of them work with magnets, but the older the machine, the longer you are likely to be in there for. Also, some machines are more sensitive than others. In some hospitals, I needed to wear a gown, and have a metal-detector passed over me, because some fabrics can contain traces of metal, which would be detected by the machine. Other machines were less sensitive, and I was simply told to not wear anything metal in my head (earrings) and to remove my watch. If having to change/strip off worries you, ask what will be necessary before you attend for an MRI. (But do leave your watch at home, because the machine can mess with the settings!)

Being inside an MRI machine is mainly boring. I found it helped to have something to think about, and you can plan this ahead. You can decide to recite poetry, or tell yourself a story, or test your multiplication tables. Anything that will help you to think about something other than not being able to move.

Sometimes they offer you music to listen to, or suggest you bring your own CD. I have absolutely *no* idea why they do this, as it's much too noisy to hear anything.

Sometimes they're cold, so if the staff offer you a blanket, it might be worth accepting it.

I hate being in confined spaces, so I always shut my eyes and kept them shut the entire time I was in the machine. However, most MRI machines seem to have an angled mirror, so you can see into the room while you're in there. You also have a button to hold, which you can press if you need to be let out suddenly. You wear headphones, partly because it's very noisy and they protect your ears, and partly so the staff can talk to you.

Most staff are very kind, they tell you you're "doing really well" (even though you are just lying there—hard to get that wrong I'd have thought). They'll also tell you how long each image will take, and when you're nearly finished. Others are less helpful, and most of them look (to me) like they're ten years old, but that's just life.

As I wrote in my diary, MRI and CT scans are slightly different. I was told that a CT scan uses 13 times the amount of radiation of a normal X-ray, so are not something you want to have regularly. They also tend to make colloid cysts 'shine', so any measurements should be considered estimates, not absolutes. (This caused me a lot of angst initially, as I couldn't understand how a cyst I had been told was 8mm could suddenly become 4mm.)

The rules about injecting dye tend to change. At my first MRI they simply injected it. Subsequent scans, I was told to first have a blood test and take the results when I went for the scan. My cyst did not enhance with contrast—in other words, the dye made no difference. I didn't enjoy being injected with dye for no reason, so asked them not to. Remember, it is your body. If you don't want something to happen, ask if it is necessary and if not, you have the right to refuse it. I was however, told that sometimes tiny cysts behave differently, so if they are checking for a possible regrowth, it is worth having.

The person doing the MRI will tell you nothing afterwards, so don't expect to be given any results. My understanding (because I asked) is that *if* they spot something unexpectedly imminently life-threatening, they will delay your departure and call for a doctor, who will discuss options with you. But in nearly every instance, you will get dressed, go home, and wait for an appointment with your doctor to discover what they saw. Sometimes this is a frustratingly long time. Try to be patient, and remind yourself, if the medics aren't in a panic, you are probably not going to die today, so you may as well enjoy it.

Chapter Three
Diary of a Brain Tumour

23rd June 2014

I am in a rather bizarre situation. I went to see my doctor because I think my hormones are unsettled. I actually saw a locum, as my doctor is on maternity leave.

One symptom is a headache which simply will not go. She listened while I described the pain being in the top of my head, that they are worse when I first get up but I am not confused or sick. She said that I should have an emergency MRI. I explained to her that I have had these headaches for years, my usual GP said not to worry about them; but she still thought I should have it checked.

Anyway, when I got home I was phoned by the NHNN. Apparently the doctor had called them and asked if I could be checked by someone in Mr M's team. It seems a bit strange. My guess is that after seeing me she did an online search for colloid cysts (or the doctor's equivalent) because she'd never heard of them before, and read all the potentially scary details. She then felt slight panic and called my consultant to get it checked. It will be a hassle to go to London, and I'm so tired at the moment, but I guess I'll go.

25th June 2014

I went to NHNN and was seen by a Mr. H. I've never seen him before, and I think he'd been asked to fit me in as an emergency appointment, because I was told to have the CT scan, and then ask reception to phone for Mr. H and he would meet me for a consultation. All felt very melodramatic and unnecessary.

I had a CT scan because the 'emergency' MRI will happen in three weeks' time, and the NHNN team wanted something to look at before they assessed me. After the scan, the radiologist asked if I was having stents fitted today or at a future date. Bit of a strange comment. Perhaps that's what usually happens when they've been asked to fit in an unscheduled scan. I told him that I hoped to never have stents fitted, which he didn't really respond to. He checked I was seeing a consultant today, before I went home. Bit weird.

Went to go and see Mr. H. Luckily I didn't have to wait long. He showed me my previous MRI and explained that the cyst was very small (about 8.5mm) and there was no sign of hydrocephalus. All of which I had heard many times before. I know that the size they tell me fluctuates, depending on who has measured it, and whether it is a CT scan or an MRI, so the size he mentioned didn't bother me—I thought perhaps he was looking at my first CT scan, and that had been measured at about 8mm.

I told him that I was very comfortable with them monitoring the cyst, and had no desire for anyone to start fiddling with my brain.

I described my latest headaches, which now were actually much better and not so severe. They are a bit different, as they are pretty much continuous (and have been for months now). I also mentioned that when I looked at my feet the pain was MUCH worse, to the extent that it made me stagger.

However, I was still able to function normally, am perfectly able to clean out the chickens, walk the dogs, cook lunch for 30 elderly people and teach English to Chinese people; so all was fine and I was impatient to leave.

Mr H then showed me another scan, and showed me the clear signs of what fluid pressing on the brain would look like. I assume this was a different patient's scan, and felt rather sorry for them. They clearly had some tough times ahead. However, I could see clear differences between that and my own scan which he'd shown me at the beginning, so I agreed that nothing needed to be done. (To be honest, I am a bit past the stage of them having to continually prove to me that I don't need an operation, but I obviously wasn't making that clear. Perhaps because I'm so tired.)

I asked if I should cancel the 'emergency MRI' as I am obviously okay. He looked a little confused and said no, I should definitely have it and he would like to see me afterwards. It seems rather unnecessary, but I thanked him and left.

When I got home, I told David nothing has changed, all is stable, but they want me to have the MRI anyway, and then go back to see them. David asked why I have to go back, and I told him I don't know. Mr. H is quite young, perhaps he's never seen a colloid cyst before and wants to write about it in a thesis or something.

2nd July 2014

I went back to NHNN today. Unexpected. I still haven't had the 'emergency' MRI.

I received a phone call from Ms. M, a senior consultant, to say that she was concerned that I had not understood her colleague (Mr. H) and she would like me to come in and discuss surgery. This was quite a shock! I was in Costa with Mum and Will when the call came and could not really concentrate on the conversation after that. I didn't want to say anything to them—because possibly they have muddled me up with someone else or something, but it was very unsettling.

David came with me this time. (I obviously missed something at the last appointment.)

Anyway, it transpires that the scan with the fluid on the brain, the second one Mr. H showed me, was actually mine! Although the cyst has not really grown and is now only about 9mm, it seems to be causing hydrocephalus. Perhaps it's moved slightly. Ms. M said that potentially this is dangerous and the cyst might have to be removed. They will know more after the 'emergency MRI' which is next week.

I feel weirdly excited! I guess it must be adrenaline but is partly due to the possibility that at long last my headaches and cyst are being definitely linked and they might be able to do something. David and I discussed the options. Surgery seems grim and potentially life threatening but so does leaving it. We decided to follow whatever the team at NHNN recommend. I am really praying that they do recommend something and won't just tell us that they *could* operate but it is up to us to decide if it is necessary or not.

11ᵗʰ July

We went to an uncle's funeral. I was able to tell my family about possibly have surgery. My sister is also in England at the moment, having arrived from Canada for a holiday.

I had to drive from Kent to Hertfordshire, and it was really hard work. I had to ask Mum not to chat, because I was having real trouble concentrating. Plus there's something wrong with my ears, there's a time delay on people talking and me hearing (it's like watching a film when the sound is running out of sync).

When we arrived in Letchworth, David met us (he was returning from work in New York). I was *so* happy to be able to handover the driving to him. The funeral went okay I think, and it was nice to be able to tell my cousins afterwards that I might have to have surgery. Cousin who's a nurse, was able to tell me what might happen during the op. It sounds grim, so I hope she's wrong.

16th July 2014

David and I went to NHNN and saw both Ms. M and Mr. M—the fact that we actually saw Mr. M in person was a clue that something serious was afoot! I haven't seen him since my early, BUPA funded consultations in 2010 (I am now a NHS patient, because we have not used BUPA to fund 'monitoring' of the condition).

Mr. M showed us all the recent MRI scans and explained how the cyst had appeared to be stable and there was no fluid around the brain, but the latest scans showed that this had changed. He said that the headaches I described were clearly linked to a build-up of fluid and in his view the cyst should now be removed.

It seemed churlish to point out that my headaches are unchanged. Clearly the internal situation is not. Plus you do not want to challenge someone who is about to cut into your brain! But I know the pain is the same pain I've been trying to describe to them since before I was even diagnosed with the cyst.

I mentioned that on the internet I had read many stories about people who either died during surgery, or were left mute, paralysed or with serious complications such as epilepsy. I asked Mr. M, of the colloid cysts that *he* had operated on, how many patients had died or had complications. And had he operated on lots previously?

He replied that he had not operated on lots, because they didn't see colloid cysts very often, but he had operated on a few. He said that none of the patients had been left with serious problems after surgery. None.

I therefore felt that I had no decision to make. I agreed to have the surgery. I asked if it could be in September, after our holiday. Mr. M said no, it needed to be done quickly.

David asked if there was any advantage in using BUPA. Mr. M said that it would be the same surgeons in the same operating room, but it was easier for him to get theatre time when working under BUPA, and I would have a nicer 'hotel' experience. We agreed that David would get a BUPA code and we would go ahead when Mr. M had got space in the theatre.

Left the hospital and had breakfast in a cafe. I texted the children and Mum, and my brother, and sister. All feels surreal.

22nd July

Tomorrow I go in for the operation. All I can really do is trust God, but I think I am ready. I love my family, and I love my life, and I don't want to die. But if my death is what God wants, if actually there are things that would happen, good things, which would only be possible without me, then I can accept that. I have got to the point where I can honestly pray, "Your will be done". I trust that if God lets me die, he'll look after my family for me, and make something good come from my death. And I trust Him to carry me safely from this life to the life He has prepared for me. It is, after all, where I was always intended to be (just a bit sooner than I had planned!)

I keep thinking of a quote by C.S. Lewis: "You don't have a soul. You *are* a soul, you have a body." I am clinging on to that thought. I remember reading a sermon by him, where he describes our life like that of an egg. Inside the egg, a duck is developing. It is protected by the shell and the white, fed by the yolk. But in order to fly and swim, to be what it is intended to be, it must at some point be released from the egg, it must hatch. If I am a soul, at some point I must be released from my body, so I can be what I was intended to be. Which is very scary, because I don't want to leave everything that I know, all the people who I love, my life as it is. But if that is what God knows is what is best, then it will be.

I think I am too scared to even be nervous, it almost feels exciting. I have prepared as much as I can, though there hasn't been much time.

I have booked another cleaner to come in and help keep the house tidy, and someone to walk the dogs. Milly and Molly (kittens from a farm) are still living in the garage, and they'll just have to stay there until I'm well enough to sort them moving outside. Unfortunately I've hatched quite a few birds this year, so David will have to cope with 25 ducks and 8 new chickens (which I don't even know if they're cockerels or hens yet, they're so young). But there's nothing I can do about that.

I have told all the groups I work with that I don't know when I'll be back, and cancelled teaching in the Chinese restaurant. After the operation I can't drive for at least 6 months, so I wouldn't be able to get there, even if I felt well enough. Everything I've read so far says it takes a year to start feeling normal again. I'm sure that's a pessimistic view, but it seems sensible to be cautious, just in case.

One good tip from the Braintalk Communities group was to write down all my pin numbers, because I'm likely to forget them. I've given them all to David, in case I also can't remember where I put the list. Losing my memory worries me. I'm taking some photos of the family and some Blutac, so when I wake up they'll be the first thing I see. I hope, so very much, that I will remember who everyone is.

My brother phoned me, and an uncle, and several friends. It was nice of them, made me feel like I wasn't going through all this on my own, and nor were my family.

I have packed my bag, but I don't know what to take. I phoned the hospital, and they said they'd emailed a list, but I can't find it, so I think they forgot. I've bought some silk scarves for afterwards, to hide the bald patch. Ms. M said they wouldn't shave my whole head, just a bit down one side, so it might not show too much.

I also went through this diary, and burnt some of the pages! I tend to write in it most often when I'm angry or upset, and some of the things I've written might hurt people if they read them, and I don't even feel those things now, so it seemed prudent to destroy them. Just in case.

There are a few meals in the freezer for when I'm in hospital, but to be honest, I haven't really felt up to cooking. I think everyone will be okay without me for a while. My sister's still here, which is brilliant, as she can take care of Mum, so that's one thing I don't need to worry about. I have written letters to David and the children, just in case, and hidden them in my bedside cabinet. It all feels very unreal.

6th August

Well, I am home. Still alive!

That was all such a bizarre experience.

On 23rd July, I caught the train to London, then walked to the hospital (I fancied some exercise in the sunshine while I had the opportunity). Will came with me, and carried my case. It was nice having someone else there, though as soon as I was in the hospital it was fine, so I told him he could go home (being in hospital is always grim, even if you're not the patient). My room was nice, and had its own bathroom.

I was a bit paranoid about catching some kind of 'superbug' (I had hydrocephalus at this point, so am using that as my excuse). Anyhow, in my suitcase, I had smuggled a cloth and a bottle of Dettox spray. After the nurse left me in my room, I shut the door, and sprayed anywhere that I thought my head might touch after the operation, and all the door handles. I was terrified in case the nurse caught me and told me off, but no one saw. It all *looked* clean, and the cloth I wiped it with didn't get dirty, so I guess it was already clean, but I felt better for having done it.

A doctor came (she looked about 10 years old) and asked me lots of questions. Then she said she needed to attach some stickers to my head, which they would use during the operation as a sort of map. This involved shaving my hair. She was very sweet about it, but it did feel a bit weird. I had assumed I would be asleep when my head got shaved. She didn't shave much, just patches, all round my head. Then she stuck on round stickers (which were like the pads you can stick on chair legs to stop them scratching the floor—but probably not those). She drew around each one with a marker pen. Being drawn on also felt odd, was weirdly dehumanising. She

70

told me not to wash my hair, as it was important they stayed in place. I wasn't really worried about them falling off, because each one had a bald patch under it, so they'd be easy enough to replace if necessary.

After this, a porter came, and said he'd come to take me for an MRI. He was quite jolly, and chatted while we walked. We had to go down in a public lift, and then across Queens Square to get to the MRI machine. I felt embarrassed being in public, it felt like people were staring at me. I had long strands of shorn hair all over my clothes, and stickers all round my head, and I didn't want to be seen in public. But I figured other people have to put up with worse.

At some point during the evening the anaesthetist came to see me. He told me when I should stop eating, and what time I should stop drinking. He said I didn't have to stay in hospital all evening, and if I wanted to go out for dinner with David I could, though I shouldn't drink wine after a certain time. He was nice, and I trusted him and felt better after I'd seen him.

I asked him about the after-effects of anaesthetic, saying I had heard that it stayed in the system for weeks afterwards, and can cause nightmares and things. He laughed! He said that surgeons chop up the body and cause all sorts of things to be unbalanced, and then afterwards, when the patient is having problems with something, the surgeon always says it's due to the anaesthetic. He said that the anaesthetic leaves the body more or less as soon as he stops administering it, and any problems afterwards, I should blame on the surgeon. (I'm not sure if that is true or not, but it made me laugh when he said it.)

David came, and spent the evening with me. Then I tried to sleep. It wasn't very easy, because hospitals don't really shut down for the night, and people kept arriving with forms to sign, or to check my blood pressure and things. The worst was at about 11.30pm, when the door crashed open, the light was switched on, and a young doctor told me I needed to sign the consent form. He then listed all the grim things that might happen to me—like dying, being paralysed, being mute—and asked me to sign the form saying that I understood. His attitude was terrible! It was so bad, it made me smile, just at the appallingness of it all. He then asked why I was smiling, didn't I realise how serious it was? I hope he was a student, and he has learned a lot since that night. It was late, he had possibly been awake for many hours, perhaps he was going to become a brilliant surgeon. Let's hope so.

The next morning seemed to last forever, and I was worried in case an emergency came in and I lost my theatre slot. I was given a bottle of pink stuff, and told to have a shower with it. Some kind of disinfectant. It said on it that it shouldn't be used for brain surgery, so I went back and checked with the nurse, but she said as I wasn't washing my hair, it would be fine, and they always used it. I had to wear an awful hospital gown, with a second one put on backwards so I didn't flash at everyone when I walked around. And support stockings, which were dark green and completely horrible.

I don't remember much else. I do remember walking down to the operating room, which was the most terrifying walk ever. I had to leave David at the door, and walk in by myself. I knew God was with me, I felt wrapped up in a warm cocoon. But it was still terrifying.

There were lots of young people in there, I guess students, all full of adrenaline and excitement and confidence. I sat on a bed, and they started asking questions and sorting stuff, and attaching me to things. Then the anaesthetist arrived, and I was so glad to see him, and said I wanted very much to be asleep. But he said they needed to sort some things first. It seemed a long time to wait. Then he said it was time, and gave me an injection.

The last thing I remember is Mr. M arriving, and I was given a mask to cover my face, and I remember holding it, and he said, "Is the patient going to hold her own mask?" and one of the students reached over and held it for me.

Then I slept.

*

I woke up to a nurse calling my name. She asked me various questions and asked me to move my arms and legs. David was there, and when she asked me what day it was, I didn't know, because I didn't know how long I'd been asleep for, but David said it was the same day.

I slept a lot. I remember images of things, like a man with a bandage around his head arriving in the bed opposite me, and he kept asking if some woman was alright—so I think he'd been in an accident (they never answered him, so I'm not sure that she was). I remember seeing my children there, and always David, and the nurse who kept waking me up, and an alarm that kept going off. I didn't feel any pain, just sleepy. I asked David to take a photo of my head, because I wanted to see if I had a big bandage like the man opposite. But I didn't, I just had a strip of plaster. They had shaved a 2 inch strip, from front to back, and covered it with a white sticker. It wasn't an attractive look, I'm not sure it will catch on.

At some point they wheeled me back to my room. I was still very sleepy. Sometimes I woke with a headache, and they gave me painkillers. (But I had been expecting a massive headache, and I never had one—perhaps I was just too used to pains in my head by then.) I was sick a lot, and couldn't eat.

73

They did give me anti-sickness tablets, but sometimes I didn't ask for them in time. A nurse came to speak to me, and told me that I *must* use my buzzer thing and call for the nurse if I had any pain or felt queasy, because they could give me something before it got bad, But I didn't like to, it felt rude to call them away from what they were doing.

Before the operation, I had been worried about sneezing afterwards, or jolting my head in case I dislodged something important. After surgery, I sneezed a few times, and was sick a lot, but my brain seemed to stay in place.

I decided to send the photo of my wound to Mum, so she would know what to expect when she came to visit me. I don't know why I sent it to a lot of other people too. When Betty was there, she checked my phone, and was a bit surprised by what I'd sent. She sent some explanatory texts to various people, explaining that I had recently had brain surgery and was in bit of a muddle. Then she told me it might be best to not text anyone until I was less fuzzy.

Mostly, having my phone was brilliant. Every time I was worried, I texted my cousin, the nurse, and she gave me helpful information. I received lots of texts from friends and relatives, and generally kept up with what was happening in the outside world. It helped me feel supported, and not alone. One friend said she'd been checking Betty's Facebook, and when she saw there were posts moaning about lots of flowers arriving at the house, she knew I must have survived!

There were a few odd things that happened. I got up at one point, to get my phone. Of course, I was attached to all sorts of tubes, but I'd forgotten, so ended up in a tangle. I had to call for a nurse, who didn't seem surprised to find her patient half out of bed with tubes and wires all in a tangle, so perhaps it happens a lot.

Then I lost something, I think a book, and thought I must've left it in my other room. David and Will were there at the time, and asked what other room? I explained that when I arrived, they were cleaning my room, so I had been asked to wait in a different one. I'd sat on the bed, and watched Will pacing up and down, which made me feel guilty for making him stressed. The nurse assured me I had never been in another room, but I remembered it very clearly, so I knew it was true. I even knew where it was, just along the corridor. They said I could go and look, so I did. It was a cupboard. Which was very strange because I *remembered* being in there. I still do.

Another memory was when Mr. M said I needed to have another MRI, to check all was well. I told him I'd already had one since the operation, why did I need another one? David assured him he had been with me the entire time, and I had *not* had an MRI. But I remembered it, very clearly.

"I know I have," I said, "because it was the same porter who came to get me. He arrived, and said hello, and told me that this time I could travel in style and go in a wheelchair." It was absolutely true.

Except it wasn't. When Mr. M went to check my records, it showed I had not been for a post op MRI. And actually, I *can't* have been, because when I did go down, the doctor who wheeled me there checked me for metal, and I had plaited my hair for the operation, and the hairbands had tiny metal blobs on them, so she had to take them off.

Apparently, air bubbles in the brain can take a *thought*, and connect it to the *memory* part of the brain, so we remember things we only thought about. (This is not a very scientific explanation, but it's how I understand it!) It was very weird, and rather disorientating. If I couldn't trust my brain any more, what could I trust?

There were a few nasty things post op. One was the injection nurse, who came to give me injections in my stomach. I know (because I texted my cousin the nurse) that they were to stop me getting blood clots, and therefore necessary, but they were awful. I hated that whenever someone came into the room, you never knew if it was going to be a visitor or a nurse with another injection. (In fact, on my last day, when I was all packed up and ready to go, and David had gone to collect the car, someone came and knocked on the door, and I told Betty to keep very quiet and pretend we had gone, in case it was the injection nurse. Betty was a bit shocked by this, and told me I should have the injection if necessary. But she did take pity on me, and we hid until the nurse had gone!)

Another nasty thing was when they came to flush out the tubes going into my arm, because it kind of stretched the veins, and hurt. The following week, my whole arm was bruised.

The very worse thing was when they took out the tube in my head. After the operation, they left a tube, going from inside my brain, out the top of my head. I think it's in case of fluid building up, so they can do something fast in an emergency. I looked like one of the Teletubbies. Obviously it had to come out before I could go home, so a young doctor came to do it. She sent David out the room, and a nurse came to hold my hand, so I guessed it wasn't going to be pleasant. The tube removal bit wasn't too bad, mainly odd, but the stitches in the top of the head weren't much fun. They couldn't use any painkiller—I guess because it was so close to the brain. It *hurt*. I listened to a tape in Mandarin, and tried to distract myself. Afterwards, the doctor thanked me for not swearing at her, which I thought was rather sad. Tough to have a job where you are abused for helping someone.

There were nice things about being in hospital too, mainly because I felt very supported. David was there pretty much all the time, and my children visited too. So did a Spanish girl. I have absolutely no idea who she was, but it was kind of her to come. My sister brought Mum to visit. It was when the book benches were in London, so she took loads of photos of them, and sent me lots of funny texts. My brother and his wife came, and a close friend. I also texted cousin-the-nurse lots, whenever I was worried about something, and that was a great support. So were texts from friends and family, it made me feel less isolated.

The staff were, of course, wonderful. I think you have to be very special to work in a hospital. However, I very much wanted to go home. I wanted to know when the door opened, it wasn't going to be the injection nurse. I wanted to turn off the light at bedtime and not be disturbed. I wanted my own bed.

I was discharged on Monday 30th July.

Before I left, I was visited by an occupational therapist, who had to check I was able to cope when out of hospital. She took me to a special room, where there was a kitchen, and asked me to cook some pasta while she watched. It was incredibly hard remembering the order of everything— saucepan full of water, on stove, add heat, wait until boils, add pasta, time for 15 minutes, strain, add sauce. You wouldn't believe the mental effort involved, it was by far the hardest thing I have ever cooked. So much of my mental energy and emotion went into that pasta. Then, when it was finished, she threw it away!

I had texted David, and told him that I could be discharged, but first I had to cook some pasta. Of course, after the invisible room and non-existent MRI incident, he thought I was talking rubbish again. But I did get home eventually.

Being home is wonderful. And scary. I hadn't realised how much security there was health-wise in hospital, how they were constantly checking my blood pressure, bringing medication, watching me. Now I am on my own, and I feel very insecure. Obviously I'm not physically on my own, my family is here, but it's up to me to alert them if something is wrong. Every twinge, every buzz in my ears, is a worry.

There's still a lot of fluid in my head, and this has come down, swelling my forehead and then my nose. I look like a centaur. It's also had a strange effect on my ears, and all voices sound like Dalek voices. The top of my head feels bruised too—like it was before the operation, when I'd had hydrocephalus. It's all very worrying. A mixture of online research, texts to cousin-the-nurse and common sense lets me know all is normal. But I feel very fragile. I have been brave enough now.

I've had more visitors now I'm home. My brother came with sweet peas from his garden, friends have popped in with fruit, or magazines, or just to chat. It's so nice to see people again, everyone is very kind. I get tired though, after about ten minutes I find it hard to concentrate on what they're saying. I hope no one thinks I'm rude, or not listening to them.

7th August

Had a good cry this morning. Feel a bit better now.

Am starting to do little jobs around the house, though it's an effort, because I start something and then get distracted. Today I washed the bedding, and marinated some chicken. I cannot face another ready-meal.

I'm beginning to need less help. When I first got home, I kept repeating things—like whole conversations (I know because the kids told me).

I also forgot what I'd just done, so taking pills was bit of a risk, because I would take them, and instantly forget whether I'd taken them or not. So Will monitored me, he would set an alarm for when I needed to take pills, watch me take them, and write it down. He's still doing this, but actually, I think I could manage on my own now, as long as I wrote it down (because I might still forget, but not quite so quickly).

Yesterday we went out to a restaurant, as it's my sister's last evening. It's so good she's been here, and it's really sad she has to go home again. It felt odd being out in public. I wore one of the scarfs I'd bought, so no one could see my scar, but I felt very 1960s. It was also odd being treated normally again, no one was 'careful' around me, I was just another customer in the restaurant. I almost wanted to tell everyone, to let them know I've just had brain surgery. (It was a bit like after having the first baby, when it consumed all my thoughts and was all I wanted to talk about.)

Some orchids arrived this morning. They are beautiful. Flowers are such a lovely gift, they are so full of colour, and I felt starved of colour in the hospital. It was very beige. I've had lovely gifts from people—flowers and plants, and books and chocolates. Even cards and gifts from the friends of my children, which is so sweet of them (mothers don't usually expect to be noticed!) It really cheers me up. So do visits, it is so kind of people to come. Lots of friends have arrived with fruit. I will associate cherries with my operation forever I think! So will Will, who is continually having to offer them to visitors before they go off, because there are way too many to eat. (I do like cherries though.)

Linda, who was helping me clean, is ill, so unable to come this week. The house is very untidy, which is depressing. I cannot summon the energy to do enough to make a difference. (I feel very dizzy soon after starting to do anything physical, and am completely exhausted after about ten minutes of work.) Simple things like opening the cupboard and removing the vacuum cleaner, and remembering how to plug it in (after finding the socket) are surprisingly difficult. But a messy house is depressing. Sue popped in today, to walk the dog, and she swept the kitchen for me. I was so grateful. I know everyone is doing lots extra, covering for the things I can't do (which is pretty much everything) so it feels ungrateful to complain. I hope I recover soon, I hate being incapable.

Chapter Four
Recovering After a Craniotomy

For the first few weeks after my op, I was fuzzy. Very fuzzy. A sort of *"I have drunk too many glasses of wine and can't quite concentrate"* sort of fuzzy. I could speak and behave relatively normally, so people didn't really notice, but processing information was an effort. It wasn't unpleasant actually, I just didn't get much done.

During this time, at the end of August, we had our family holiday. David and I had to drive, rather than fly, because brain surgery causes air bubbles in the brain, and you can't fly until they have gone. The holiday was excellent, mainly because it gave my family a chance to relax, they didn't have to look after me and the house, and *they* could recover from the stress of my surgery. Brain surgery impacts the whole family, and we shouldn't forget that.

When the fuzz finally cleared (after a few weeks) I was mainly tired. I also found that I became anxious very easily and was very emotional. Anything that would normally have made me think, "Aw, that's sad" now made me cry. Sometimes it was hard to stop crying. Close friends and family became accustomed to seeing me with a red nose and I carried tissues wherever I went. Initially, I found this intensely embarrassing. Then I began to notice that actually, no one minded and many people actual preferred the 'weak' me. There is a lot of competition in life, a lot of keeping up of appearances. It is a strain on everyone. Most people were very comfortable with the scatty red nosed lady who now attended things. I became closer friends with a lot of people. Mostly, people are nice.

However, to be honest, some people—often those I expected to be supportive—were sometimes hurtful. It was almost like they were jealous of the help/attention I was receiving, especially in the first days of being at home, when I was unable to do anything. People would make comments about me being "like Lady of the manor, resting all day," or tell me that, "if you want to know something that heals really slowly, you should try breaking your wrist." I am sure they didn't mean to be nasty, that probably they spoke without thinking, or were trying to jolly me along. But it was unexpected, and it was hurtful. I mention it because I know other people have suffered similar hurts, and I want to warn you. People do not always react how we think—but try not to take it personally, and focus on all the people who are amazing and kind and do so much more than you ever dreamed they would to help you.

I always covered my scar when I left the house, or if we had visitors. It was a good scar, and I was secretly rather proud of it. About a week after I got home, I went to my local surgery, and a nurse removed the stitches. It didn't hurt at all. I was left with a rather fine 'pirate scar' across my head. However, other people might be less impressed, or even squeamish, so until my hair grew back I covered it. I only once uncovered it in public, which was while we were driving to Italy in August, and I needed to adjust my scarf in front of a mirror in the ladies' washroom. A couple of women were using the sinks, and they stared at me in horror. I kept it covered after that.

It seems that head wounds do bother some people. I went for a routine MRI recently (I think I will always need to have MRI checks now, just to be sure nothing has regrown). The nurse asked how big the titanium plate was, which had been screwed onto my skull. I said I had no idea, but she could feel if she wanted to check, because you can feel a sort of outline in the lumps on my skull. She put out her hand, felt the dips and bumps, squealed and jumped away! I laughed, and told her I didn't think she was supposed to react like that. She was very embarrassed, and apologised repeatedly, but it does show that even medics are perhaps not used to repaired skulls, so perhaps we should be sensitive around hairdressers, and other people who may have to deal with them.

However, there is another, opposite view to this—so you might disagree. Having a head wound is nothing to be ashamed of, and perhaps the pressure today to conform is too great. Maybe we should be happy to let others see our scars. As I write this, I am about to attend a fashion show, organised by ActionAid, where all the models are women who have facial scars from acid attacks. They feel they want to be seen, that people should become accustomed to faces that do not fit the 'perfect' image we try to project. Perhaps they are right. I don't know (I just know that personally, I don't want my scar to be the thing people remember about me).

*

After about six months, I began to feel that I was finally 'getting better'. My hair had grown back (my surgeon was a rubbish hair stylist—more a 'shave down one side' than a style) and I could stop wearing the annoying scarves over my bald patch. The scar still had no hair, but it was completely hidden by a 'comb over'. I was also able to dye it again. (I was allowed to wash it after the stitches were removed, but only with baby shampoo for about three months, as the wound was sensitive.)

All my 'unrelated to the cyst' headaches stopped after the craniotomy. I did still have headaches, and immediately after surgery I had lots. But they were normal headaches, the sort that disappeared if I took paracetamol. Does this prove the constant migraines were related to the cyst? Well, maybe not. I guess it could be argued that while I had the cyst, my general stress levels were increased, which caused migraines. Or perhaps when they cut through my brain, something else became rebalanced, hence causing the migraines to stop.

But I am not a scientist, I am an author, and for me, it was all the proof I needed that those migraines were caused by the colloid cyst. I do sometimes have nasty pains in my head—not migraines, but something that almost feels like the bones are knitting together (which I don't think it can be) and one neurosurgeon said that he thought they were just the effects of having had brain surgery. They don't last very long, just a few hours, so I'm not complaining.

I still got tired very easily, especially if I was doing 'brain stuff.' So I could only read, write, hold a conversation, for a limited amount of time before I felt exhausted. It is very difficult to rest a brain, and activities we usually associate with rest—like watching television or reading—are actually exhausting. All that mental stimuli, lights and noise, uses up lots of brain energy.

I wasn't physically tired though and a walk across the fields or pottering around in the garden, gave my brain enough rest to then start working for another stint. It was important to recognise what was tired (my brain) and what was fine (my body) so I could still do things, just mentally demanding things needed to be paced correctly. It is important to do as much as we can, partly because it's not fair on other people to be more of a burden than we need to be, partly because unless we try to do things, we won't know if we can.

I also still had memory issues. That Christmas, I did cook the normal big Christmas turkey dinner with all the trimmings. However, it only happened because my son stood next to me, reminding me of what I was doing. He would say things like: "There's a saucepan of water boiling, did you mean to put those sprouts into it? When did you last check the sausages? Are those breadcrumbs for the stuffing?"

He didn't actually need to *do* anything, but he did the thinking bits for me. Without him, I would happily have boiled saucepans of water while the vegetables sat on the side. I'm not sure if this was because it was the right side of my brain that was damaged, or if brain surgery in general causes this. Nothing was 'automatic' anymore. I think being aware of the stage of recovery is important, asking for the help that is needed while doing as much as possible yourself. Doing things made me feel more confident; having help, meant that I could actually achieve what I wanted to.

One good thing, is that I can reread novels and watch old movies, and I have absolutely no idea what the ending will be. Even today, several years after surgery, I can still watch something I think is new, and then half way through I start to recognise the plot and realise I have watched it before. It's rather nice to enjoy things for a second time.

Driving was another issue. There is no way, straight after surgery, that I was alert enough to drive, so being banned was fine. However, after a few months I felt much better, and began the tedious process of trying to get my licence back. The rules will be different for different countries, but in England, it is quite complicated. You can look online for the current rulings—and it is worth doing this before surgery. If you are having a craniotomy, you cannot drive for six months post op. If you voluntarily submit your licence, it is much easier to get it back afterwards. If you don't, eventually the hospital have to tell the DVLA, who will cancel your licence. Getting a cancelled licence reinstated takes much longer. So write a letter, explaining the situation, and send them the licence before surgery. (Do check this, it might have all changed.)

However, getting the licence returned was still an issue. Part of the problem seems to be that the insurance companies want the surgeon to say when someone is fit to drive. The surgeons (quite correctly in my opinion) are unwilling to do this (because then they can be held liable by the insurance companies). So a surgeon will be prepared to give an assessment of your health, but not actually say, "Therefore this person is fit to drive". That is the job of the DVLA.

I tried to find out from the DVLA when my licence would be returned. They seem to be in perpetual chaos. When the six month ban is completed, they then begin the slow process of writing to the doctor to confirm your recovery, and completing the paperwork to return the licence. I read stories of people waiting months and months beyond the six month ban before their licence is returned.

The DVLA had a 'help-line', which no one ever answered. As in, not ever. My husband even rang a different department of the DVLA on a different pretext, and chatted to someone who confirmed that no one was ever assigned to that helpline. This has been such a problem, that the government has actually passed a ruling, which says that if you do not know of any reason why you cannot drive, then you can, even if your licence has not been reissued. (Article 88) I found this online, and printed it off, so that if I happened to be stopped by the police, I could show them why I was unable to produce my licence. I also asked my surgeon to write a letter, saying I had made a good recovery, and I put that in the car too.

I had informed my car insurance company prior to surgery (which meant I wasn't paying unnecessarily while unable to drive) and I also told them when I intended to start driving. *Do not drive until the insurance company has agreed they will cover you.* As I mentioned above, this was far from simple. In the end, we came up with some wording which my surgeon was prepared to write, and the insurance company were prepared to accept, in order to insure me.

However, when insurance is in place, if your surgeon says you are well enough to drive, then my understanding is that you can. Even if your licence has not been returned (as long as you submitted it and did not have it disqualified).

I was able to drive again after six months, as I had no complications post op. My licence was not returned for several months after this date. As I live in a rural location, not being able to drive was both inconvenient and expensive (due to taxi fares). I definitely began to feel more human when I could drive again.

After about nine months, I felt as if I had improved as much as I was going to, though I still got in muddles easily. Previously, I had been a primary school teacher. When teaching a class—sometimes of thirty children—I knew exactly where every child was in the room and roughly what they were doing. I knew which ones could work independently and which ones I needed to check on regularly to keep them on track. Any change in noise or movement, I noticed at once and could stop distractions before they happened. I could respond to questions, accidents, behavioural problems, as they happened, whilst maintaining the general calm of the classroom. All this was a lot of information to hold in my brain. Even when I felt better, I was not confident that I could juggle so much all at once.

I think the key word here is 'confidence'. It is possible that, had I needed to, I would have coped perfectly well. However,

I just wasn't sure that I would notice if a child slipped out of the room. If there HAD been an accident, even if it wasn't my fault, I would have worried that I missed something that could have avoided it. I therefore decided I would not return to teaching, not yet.

However, I was bored. A friend suggested that I started writing a blog and this led to writing longer articles and then novels. I still got mentally exhausted and had to take regular breaks, but I felt that I was achieving something. Again, I think only *you* know what *you* feel able to cope with. But if you cannot do what you did before, do something different. It is all about taking small steps on the road to recovery—and recovering from brain surgery is a very, very, long road. Brains heal MUCH slower than broken bones.

The following August, thirteen months post op, we went to Malta. My boys had bought the Game of Thrones board game. This is quite fun, not as rude as the films, and a good 'family bonding' activity. However, it also has lots of rules. Millions of them. I found that I still kept forgetting them and this was extremely frustrating. I became very angry with myself and very emotional (the whole crying thing was better by this time but still not as calm as I would have liked). I am *so* not someone who cries over board games, so that added another level of frustration. I just could not hold enough information in my head.

I'm not sure that there's a solution to this one. There are things that are simply too difficult, which would not have been a problem prior to surgery. I rather spoilt the game by bursting into tears. It would have been better to have laughed and asked for help. I think a lot of recovery is to do with being aware of when to stop, to know what will stretch and improve us, and what will simply frustrate us. The thing is, no one else will know what is hard for us. As I said earlier, if we had a broken leg, people would see the limp and walk slower for us, they wouldn't expect us to climb a mountain. Once your hair has grown back, everyone will assume that because you look 'normal', you are completely back to where you were. If you're not, it is up to you to tell them. It is okay to say, "I cannot do that anymore."

Eighteen months post op, I was cooking for forty people at a lunch club for the elderly (which was fine unless someone tried to have a conversation at the same time and then things went a little awry—but no one noticed). I was writing every morning. I was raising poultry and running the house. I seemed completely recovered.

However, even today, three years post op, I still have limited 'brain energy' —if I am in a noisy place, or chatting to people, or focussed on cooking, after about three hours, I *cannot* think. Even having a conversation is difficult. Being in a crowded room, being in an airport, going to a party, are all exhausting. I also find I cannot 'filter' sound, so when in a crowd it is almost impossible to concentrate on a conversation. My brain is bombarded with noise, and it cannot ignore any of it.

I have to be careful not to drive home after tiring events.

My sight is still very poor, because the hydrocephalus stretched the optic nerve (my feet are no longer in focus unless I wear glasses!)

I lose track of time—even where we are in the year—I have to remind myself "we've had summer, Christmas is next", and I set alarms for anything I need to be on time for.

One of my biggest struggles has been with anxiety. Leaving the house is difficult, going to a restaurant is scary, going into someone else's house is terrifying. I have no idea why, perhaps because the nerves go to my stomach, and no one wants you to be ill in their toilet.

However, this is getting better. To begin with, I only ever left the house with a supply of Immodium, spare clothes, and a lot of prayer. Gradually I have learnt that I can do things, it will be okay, if I have a panic attack (a whole new joy since surgery) then I know how to control my breathing and relax my body. And I pray—I pray in a way I never did before. As I begin to achieve more and more, as I learn to trust that God will help me to do things without my body folding up in panic, I am beginning to trust him more. It has taken time, but everything about recovery has taken time.

I now often travel, and in fact my recent novel, *CLARA*, was partly set in the slums of India, where I visited many times. As I wandered through the red-light district, talking to the people who lived there, or sat in a home in the slums, learning about people's lives, I realised that actually, by many standards, I was doing quite brave things. Recovery is slow, but eventually, we get there.

As we get older, things stop working perfectly, especially our brains. A lot of women my age forget things and get tired. There is a danger that we blame everything on our surgery. We do not know how we would be if we hadn't been ill and had major surgery. In many ways, it's not worth worrying about. We are where we are.

What's important is that we recognise where we are, and know that we still have a lot to offer—even if it's different to what we were able to give when we were younger. We have more understanding for people who are older, in pain, finding life difficult. We have had to learn patience, that we are not invincible, we have faced death and lived to tell the tale. Maybe we are better people than we were before.

When I had written this, I was chatting to my son about it, telling him what I had written. During the conversation, I made the point that if I could go back a few years, to before I was ever diagnosed with a brain tumour and was given the choice, either to have the tumour and craniotomy as happened, or to never have had either, I would choose the path I had been given. True, it was painful and emotionally difficult. But the things that I have learned about myself, the new way that I have learned to trust God, the knowledge that I have gained about other people, what it means to suffer and survive, new strengths that I never knew that I had—it has been worth it.

That is not to say I would welcome another colloid cyst, which I know is a possibility—ghastly thought! Whilst colloid cysts usually do not compare in severity to other types of brain tumour, and can usually be monitored or removed, they also have an annoying tendency to regrow. I often read about people on Facebook who are going for their second or third craniotomy, that their cysts keep regrowing. Frankly, this is awful, and I don't know how I would cope. I just have to trust that God, and the people who supported me last time, will be there in the future, whatever that future holds.

Brain surgery changes us. However, we would change anyway. Never forget that you are a valuable person, what you can offer now may not be the same as you could offer before being ill, you are different. Perhaps you are better.

****

Pre-Surgery Checklist (This will be different for everyone, but there might be some things here that you've forgotten):

1. Tell employer/children's schools/clubs what is happening. You will be out of action for a while.
2. Cancel any regular deliveries (newspapers, milk, magazines, etc)
3. Arrange for child/pet care.
4. Fill freezer with easy-cook meals for when you get home.
5. Send off your driver's licence, and write to DVLA so they know what's happening. Also inform your car insurance company.
6. Write down any pin numbers, and give them to a trusted friend. If you are the sort of person who hides a key in the garden, or jewellery in odd places, tell them that too. Otherwise you might never see those things again!
7. Plan head gear for after surgery (I felt much happier having some silk scarves to hand when visitors arrived).
8. Pack: comfortable clothes, slippers, glasses, phone and recharger, toiletries. Also worth taking lip-salve, tissues and a book. Wet wipes are nice before you can get out of bed for a wash. If you have long hair, take something to tie it back with (I plaited mine for surgery). If you take regular medication, check with the hospital about whether to take those. Plus dried prunes, liquorice, or equivalent (everyone becomes very interested in your bowel movements after surgery!)
9. If you will be in hospital for a long time, arrange for someone to collect and wash dirty clothes for you. (I had a 'reserve' bag of clothes packed ready for my daughter to

bring in after a couple of days, and swapped it for a bag of laundry.)

10. Check that any important post/bills that might arrive in the next few months are being sorted by someone else.

11. Arrange for someone to clean the house when you are home again, at least for a couple of weeks.

What I think it means to be a Christian (just in case you're interested).

Sometimes, people ask, "Do I have to go to church to be a Christian?

The short answer is clearly: "No."

I am a Christian, I have a relationship with a living God and if I were stranded on a desert island or in a country that did not allow churches, then I would still have that relationship with God. I would still be a Christian. However, the answer is not complete if left there.

I think we first need to think about why you might ask that question. Understand this, God likes you. He wants to have a friendship with you. But that involves some effort on both sides.

Maybe we first need to think about what is a Christian. What makes someone a Christian?

"Ah," you might say, "well, I believe in God."

Let's look at that for a minute.

I have been reading the book of James in the Bible. I love that book—he is so rude to people! I'm sure you know that Mary gave birth to Jesus (what we celebrate every Christmas) but you may not realise that after she had Jesus, she and Joseph then had other children. One of these was James. He grew up with Jesus, and yet it is thought that for a while he didn't believe that Jesus was special. There is even a story about Jesus preaching to people and his family coming to try and stop him because they thought he was crazy. (That gives me hope, when I get things wrong I know that so did the people who wrote the Bible but they had a second chance at getting it right.) Later, James did come to believe what Jesus was saying and at some point he wrote his book. In that book, he discusses what it means to be a Christian and he talks about people who say they believe in God. First he says: "Well done!"

Few people would dispute that just as there are good things in the world, so too there are evil influences. In the Bible these are called demons or Satan. Now, when people tell James that they believe in God, he says:

"Well done." He then adds (a little sarcastically perhaps) "So do the demons!"

You see, the Bible is very clear that these evil forces believe in God and are terrified of him, because they recognise his power. Clearly demons are *not* Christians, so there must be more to being a Christian than just believing that God is real.

Think about when your computer freezes. Something has gone wrong, nothing works properly and pressing 'escape' or 'control and delete' makes no difference. Sometimes, the only option is to shut it down and restart. Well, that is what becoming a Christian is. It is realising that we've made a mess of things, something is not working properly and we need to restart. You have a 'restart' button, you just need to ask God to press it for you!

It really is that easy. There is nothing that you can do to make things right with God, you are not big enough, clever enough or good enough. So God did it all. He became a human (in the form of Jesus) and he died and was separated from the God bit of himself, which means that we don't have to. Jesus rose up from the dead (what we celebrate at Easter time) to show that he is stronger than death, that everything is sorted out for us. We just have to ask God to press that 'restart' button to set us right.

Actually, this can be quite hard to do. We like to be in control, we like to think that what we do makes a difference, that somehow we can become good enough for God. Well, I have to tell you, the Bible is very clear, there is nothing that you can do to be acceptable to God. You are not good enough. So God did it for you.

You do have to be prepared to accept that gift though, you do have to want that 'restart' button to be pressed. If life is going well for you, that can be a bit scary. We are worried that it means loss of control, that we wont be ourselves anymore. Let me remind you of what I said at the beginning: God likes you. Really, he does! He doesn't want you to become a different person, just a better version of yourself.

You don't have to be a 'bad' person to need God. Everyone needs him. I have travelled to lots of different countries, met rich people and poor and I can honestly tell you, people are people wherever you go. I have stayed at the Savoy Hotel and been driven to St James's Palace in a fleet of silver Mercedes to have dinner with Prince Charles (this is due to who I married, nothing to do with me, in case you are mistaken into thinking I am great in any way). I have also stayed in a mud hut in Zambia with a couple who were HIV positive. I have visited China, Singapore, Dubai, India, America and most of Europe and there is one thing that I can tell you. People are the same. They might be culturally very different, but deep down, we all want the same things: we all love, we all have fears, we all make a mess of things. We all need God. It is that simple.

So, what comes next? After we have admitted that actually we might not be perfect and we want to include God in our lives, what do we have to do now?

Well, you do not have to do anything (including go to church). However, if you really have 'restarted' (and not just said the words to yourself as a sort of magic chant or insurance policy), if you really do want to include God in how you live, then that will make a difference to how you live.

A baby is alive after he's born, but he doesn't grow into a healthy child and adult unless he eats and exercises. So, just as we need to spend time with people and chat with them to develop a friendship, so too we need to spend time with God. No, this still does not have to involve going to a church! We chat with God by praying (saying things to him, either out loud or thinking them in our heads). We listen to God by paying attention to our consciences, reading the Bible (where he has given us lots of hints about what he is like) and by listening to other Christians. Ah, now we get to the church bit. How can you listen to other Christians, hear their story and share yours, if you never meet any?

It is a bit like supporting a football team. I can say I support Crystal Palace. I can buy a scarf that's the right colour, I can check the results in the newspaper, I can even watch a match on television. But it would be hard for that knowledge to touch my emotions. However, if I attend one of their games, if I stand with other supporters and cheer when they score, then just the volume and shared excitement will begin to affect me. I am helped along by other fans' enthusiasm and I actually feel part of what I say I am involved with. It is hard (and a bit boring) to be a football fan in isolation. It is the same with being a Christian.

"What constitutes a church?" you might ask. "Does it need to be in an Anglican church building, or does the church that meets in my local school count?"

Well, if we look back at the Bible, a 'church' was actually just a group of people who believed the same thing. The first Christians were actually thrown out of their synagogues (the equivalent of our church buildings) and tended to meet secretly in houses. A church is not the building, it is the people.

Sometimes buildings can be helpful. I cannot stand in a huge cathedral like St Paul's without thinking about God, all the architecture has been designed to make me feel like that. However, the building is not essential. Three people meeting in a field to talk about God, to pray and study the Bible together; that is a church.

Some people might say they don't need God, they are wrong. I think this is why Jesus talked about it being hard for a rich person to know God. When we are healthy and comfortable it can be hard to acknowledge that we need God, we think we are 'okay actually'.

Some people think they are too bad to know God, they are wrong too. God is able to press the 'restart' button for murderers, thieves, adulterers and even that nasty gossip from down the road! The Bible calls all that 'sin', but it's not a word that tends to crop up at the dinner table so I have tried to avoid using it. None of us is good enough, certainly I'm not.

That's another reason for going to a church—it will help you to realise that you are not the only bad person who God likes! Have you ever read 'Screwtape Letters' by C.S. Lewis? If not, buy a copy. It's a brilliant book, very funny but with some really poignant truths included. He talks about all the strange and ordinary people who attend church.

"Ah," you might say, "but churches are religious. I am a Christian but I don't believe in religion. Religion just causes trouble, look at all the wars that have been started by religion."

You are half right. Religion does cause trouble. That is why Jesus did not start a new religion, he just pointed people to God. He refused to set down lists of rules, he just gave people principles to live by. When churches start making lots of rules, when they are more concerned with religion than with God, then they are missing the point. Christianity is meant to be about relationship, not rules.

I am often told that, "Church is boring."

Yes, sometimes it is. If it always is, then maybe you are going to the wrong church. I would also ask you, when you go to church, what are you expecting to get out of it? If your answer is "nothing" then you are probably right, you probably will get nothing from attending. However, if you dare to go hoping that you might hear God speaking to you, then that is much more likely to happen. Sometimes it is something the speaker says, sometimes it's something in the reading that week, or a hymn that's sung, or even what the person giving out the hymn books says, but usually, if we expect God to speak, we hear him.

I would also say that just like a growing baby, we grow in faith very slowly. Sometimes it is much later that we remember something that was said in church and it helps us. But if you weren't there, you wont hear it.

If church is a collection of people, then try to find a church which has people like you in it. If you are a teenager, try to find where other teenaged Christians meet. If you are a retired person, then try to find somewhere that older Christians meet. If a church caters for all ages that is wonderful but in my experience it is rare.

Do we have to go to church on Sundays? I guess not. If you attend a school Christian Union or something similar, then that is really just another form of 'church'. We are advised though that we need one day a week that we keep as a holy day, a day to rest and where thinking about God is part of our routine (I think God knew how bad we would be at including him, so suggested that it should become part of our schedule!) That is hard to do if we attend 'church' on a week day.

What about other religions? To be honest, I don't know. As I said, Christianity is all about that 'restart' button, about including God in your life and having a relationship with him. I don't know if people can find God in other religions. I do have a sneaky suspicion that when I get to Heaven there will be a lot of people there who I wasn't expecting! Whether or not people have a relationship with God is between them and God.

What about Hell? Again, this is something that I don't know much about. If being with God makes us complete and fulfilled then I guess Hell must be the opposite of that. Sometimes people ask about who goes to Hell and what about people who try, but never knew God. I cannot say, that is between them and God. But the Bible is pretty clear that if people decide that they don't want to include God when they are physically alive, then God will respect that after they have died. That's what free will and choice is all about, even if it means terrible consequences.

So, have a think and decide what you believe. If you have never asked God to press the 'restart' button in your life, maybe now is a good time to do so. There aren't any magic words, God is God, not a genie in a bottle! You might say something like:

"God, I believe that you are real. I know that I make mistakes and I'm sorry. Please will you forgive all the things that I've done wrong. Please be part of my life. I want you to be my God."

Then, you should tell someone. We are physical beings and telling someone will help you to believe what you have done and not forget about it. Then go and find some other Christians. In England you could look for somewhere that runs an Alpha course (they tend to be churches that welcome new Christians).

Do you have to go to church if you are a Christian? Not unless you want to grow……

I hope this personal account has been helpful.

I would like to thank the staff at the NHNN in London for their advice and care and complete brilliance.

Thank you too to my family, and all my friends, who were such a great support, and who continue to be understanding when I forget things or don't talk sense. Some names have been changed.

Thank you for reading. I write a blog each week, which can be found at:

anneethompson.com

I have now written several books. Why not look for them in bookshops and Amazon?

For people who enjoy travel, or laughing, or both, I wrote ***The Sarcastic Mother's Holiday Diary.*** Described as: *"The Durrells meet Bill Bryson"* and *"A laugh-out-loud travel book."* The book shows how travelling with a tumour, and immediately after a craniotomy, are not only possible, but also rewarding.
Why not read a copy today? (You can read it for free if you have a Kindle.)

I wrote the thriller, ***Counting Stars,*** after my craniotomy, and one of the characters depicts the challenges of recovering from brain surgery.

I referred in this book to my research into psychopathy. I used this to write *JOANNA—the story of a psychopath.* It is a fast paced, gritty novel.

I then wrote *CLARA—A Good Psychopath?*
I wanted to show that someone born with the psychopathic disorder was not destined to be destructive, and in some situations, the disorder might even be a strength. The novel is set partly in India.

Explore what happens when a happily married young mother falls in love with another man, in *Invisible Jane.*

Another light read is *Hidden Faces*—which is the book I always promised myself I would write when I was a teacher. A novel, it follows three infant school teachers.

The Netherley Farm books describe the love and laughter that allow a farming family to overcome unexpected challenges. Both *Ploughing Through Rainbows* and *Sowing Promises* are heartwarming, stand-alone novels.

The book I think is my best, is the novel *Out by Ten*.

Why not read a new novel today? We all need a little fun in life. All my books are available from Amazon, and can be ordered from bookshops and libraries.

Anne E. Thompson

Also by Anne E. Thompson

Hidden Faces
Invisible Jane
Counting Stars
JOANNA
Clara Oakes

The Sarcastic Mother's Holiday Diary

Ploughing Through Rainbows
Sowing Promises

Out by Ten

See anneethompson.com for details

Printed in Great Britain
by Amazon